Praise for *People Analytics*

"*People Analytics* is a watershed book in advancing the understanding of human dynamics. No longer must we rely solely on intuition when it comes to behavior; we now have hard measures for soft skills. These advances bring what used to be nuance to the forefront in driving performance."

—**Michael Arena**, Head of Global Talent & Organization Capability, General Motors

"This is one of those rare books that combines engrossing examples, practical advice, and counter-intuitive research. Ben Waber convincingly shatters orthodoxies of team and workplace design. A must-read."

—**Scott Anthony**, Managing Partner, Innosight; author of *The Little Black Book of Innovation*

"In *People Analytics*, Ben Waber presents a thought-provoking comparison between formal organizational structures and how work actually gets done. In doing so, he provides numerous examples to illustrate how social analytics could help transform business operating practices in the future. It's a fascinating area of study."

—**Paul Mascarenas**, Chief Technical Officer, Ford Motor Company

"In *People Analytics*, Ben Waber provides us with a fresh and breathless look at how we might better design work and organizations if we were to take into account what people actually do in and out of their respective cubicles, teams, projects, and work units. This is entirely imaginable science fiction that rests on the striking results of a set of ingenious, practical, and rather persuasive field experiments that bring big data to bear on the social world. A worthy and rousing read."

—**John Van Maanen**, Professor of Organization Studies, MIT; author of *Tales of the Field*

"This is more than a required read—this is must-have workforce survival knowledge for all leaders and individual contributors. Dr. Waber takes us on an exciting journey that ends in showing how sociometric data can help all of us, from CEO to front line manager to the shop floor technician, deliver consistent winning results."

—**Gene Fraser**, Corporate Vice President, Programs, Quality and Engineering, Northrop Grumman Corporation

"Human connection is all-important and *People Analytics* gives great insight on how businesses can strengthen that connection."

—**John Hesselmann**, Bank of America Merrill Lynch, Specialized Industries Executive

"*People Analytics* is a terrific book that provides real and important insight into ways to maximize the value of the new work environment and helps us see over the horizon to understand what can be done to create the optimum enterprise of the future."

—**Tracey Edwards**, Global Chief Knowledge Officer, Deloitte

"Ben Waber follows a new trail of 'digital breadcrumbs' to see the world with fresh perspective. We know our technology shapes us; …a clearer vision may enable us to design with purpose and take a human-centered approach. A fascinating read."

—**Sherry Turkle**, Professor, MIT; author, most recently of *Alone Together: Why We Expect More of Technology and Less from Each Other*

People Analytics

People Analytics

How Social Sensing Technology Will
Transform Business and What It Tells
Us about the Future of Work

Ben Waber

Vice President, Publisher: Tim Moore
Associate Publisher and Director of Marketing: Amy Neidlinger
Executive Editor: Jeanne Glasser Levine
Editorial Assistant: Pamela Boland
Development Editor: Russ Hall
Operations Specialist: Jodi Kemper
Marketing Manager: Megan Graue
Cover Designer: Chuti Prasertsith
Managing Editor: Kristy Hart
Senior Project Editor: Lori Lyons
Copy Editor: Paula Lowell
Proofreader: WriteOrWrong Proofreading Services
Indexer: Ken Johnson
Compositor: Nonie Ratcliff
Manufacturing Buyer: Dan Uhrig

Pearson Education, Inc.
Publishing as FT Press
Upper Saddle River, New Jersey 07458

FT Press offers excellent discounts on this book when ordered in quantity for bulk purchases or special sales. For more information, please contact U.S. Corporate and Government Sales, 1-800-382-3419, corpsales@pearsontechgroup.com. For sales outside the U.S., please contact International Sales at international@pearsoned.com.

Printed in the United States of America

First Printing May 2013

ISBN-10: 0-13-315831-4
ISBN-13: 978-0-13-315831-1

Pearson Education LTD.
Pearson Education Australia PTY, Limited.
Pearson Education Singapore, Pte. Ltd.
Pearson Education Asia, Ltd.
Pearson Education Canada, Ltd.
Pearson Educación de Mexico, S.A. de C.V.
Pearson Education—Japan
Pearson Education Malaysia, Pte. Ltd.

Library of Congress Cataloging-in-Publication Data is on file.

To Becca and Josh

Contents at a Glance

Contents

Acknowledgments

A major point in this book is that we need others to succeed, and in that sense I have been luckier than most. Nearly all of the work in this book was done in close collaboration with a number of people who have inspired me and profoundly shaped my thinking.

The genesis of this book actually began when I joined Sandy Pentland's group at the MIT Media Lab. Since then, Sandy has been a tremendous advisor and mentor. Not only did he have a tremendous impact on me intellectually, but the opportunities that he helped create have also been life changing.

It was also in Sandy's group where I was paired up with Taemie Kim and Daniel Olguin. Together with Sandy, we collaborated on most of the experiments I discuss in this book. It was through our collaboration and friendship that we were able to push the boundaries of science and sensing during our time at MIT and beyond.

Other people at MIT were also huge influences, and I can't possibly thank them all. Still, I wanted to give a shout out to some people in particular: Nadav Aharony, Anmol Madan, Wen Dong, Ankur Mani, Wei Pan, Coco Krumme, Akshay Mohan, Riley Crane, Manuel Cebrian, Yves-Alexandre de Montjoye, Joost Bonsen, Lanthe Chronis, Miki Hayakawa, Koji Ara, Yasuhiro Ono, Juan Carlos Barahona, Nathan Davis, Margaret Ding, Inna Lobel, Laura Freeman, Alex Speltz, Lynn Wu, Erik Brynjolfsson, Nicole Freedman, Hiroshi Ishii, Mirei Rioux, Lily Fu, Joe Paradiso, Josh Lifton, Cesar Hidalgo, Marta Gonzalez, Amy Sun, and Everett.

My collaborators from other institutions have also been a pleasure to work with: Sinan Aral, Kazuo Yano, Norihiko Moriwaki, Daniel Oster, Peter Gloor, David Lazer, Leon Danon, Ellen Pollock, Kate Ehrlich, and Tuomas Jaanu.

My time in Japan was also transformational for me, and for that I have to thank the Kitabatakes and KCJS for giving me a new perspective on life and for creating a second home on the other side of the world.

Outside of academia, it's been amazing to work with the entire Sociometric family (the "badgers"). I can't wait to see what else we create together.

Big thanks go to my cousin, Geoff Livingston, for connecting me with Katherine Bull and eventually to Jeanne Glasser Levine, who's been an absolute pleasure to work with on this book. Additional thanks to all the people at Pearson, particularly Lori Lyons, Russ Hall, Megan Graue, and Paula Lowell. When I look back at how much you helped shape this book, I'm again reminded of how much we need others, and how we can create great things when we work with great people.

Finally, I want to thank my family: my parents, who put up with me when I was being obnoxious (always); my brother Andrew and his fiancé Ressa, who did the same; and my grandparents and extended family, who provided a stable grounding for me and always kept me focused on what really mattered.

To my wife Becca, my son Josh, and Rufus: Nothing makes me happier than to spend my time with you. Everything I've done, everything I will do, is because of you guys. I'm so lucky to have a family that likes to goof off as much as we do, debate as much as we do, and still speak so respectfully to each other. ;-)

About the Author

Ben Waber is President and CEO of Sociometric Solutions, a management services firm that uses social sensing technology. He is also a visiting scientist at the MIT Media Lab, where he received his Ph.D. He was previously Senior Researcher at Harvard Business School.

Waber's work has been featured in *Wired*, the *New York Times*, on NPR, and he has given invited talks at Google, EMC, and Samsung. His research was selected for the *Harvard Business Review*'s List of Breakthrough Ideas and the *Technology Review*'s Top 10 Emerging Technologies.

Preface

People analytics is simultaneously an extremely old and new phe-nomenon. When we use data to uncover the workplace behaviors that make people effective, happy, creative, experts, leaders, followers, connectors, early adopters, and so on, we are using people analytics. Thousands of years ago, this data came from humans' observations of the world. By watching their collaborators interact with other people and react to changing conditions, people were able to make edu-cated guesses about what makes them effective and happy. Later, we augmented our senses using surveys and interviews. These methods allowed us to obtain responses from thousands of people, establishing new metrics that were a bit more quantitative, but this did not herald any radical change in the way people run companies.

Today, people analytics is poised for a revolution, and the catalyst is the explosion of hard data about our behavior at work. This data comes from a wide variety of sources. Digital traces of activity from e-mail records, web browsing behavior, instant messaging, and all the other IT systems we use give us incredibly detailed data on how people work. Who communicates with whom? How is IT tool usage related to productivity? Are there work styles that aren't well-supported by current technology? Although this data can provide amazing insights, it's only the digital part of the story.

Data on the physical world is also expanding at a breakneck pace thanks to the rapid development of wearable sensing technology. These sensors, from company ID badges to cell phones to environ-mental sensors, provide reams of fine-grained data on interaction pat-terns, speaking patterns, motion, and location, among other things. Because most communication and collaboration happens face to face, this data is critical for people analytics to take that next leap forward and become a transformative organizational tool. By combining pre-cise data from both real and virtual worlds, we can now understand behavior at a previously unimaginable scale.

In this book, I use this data in a series of case studies to illumi-nate a new kind of people analytics. In particular, we'll see how slight changes in behavior, from changing when you take breaks to what lunch tables you sit at, can make you happier, healthier, and more productive. This book shows how people analytics transforms our understanding of socialization in the workplace, the impact of office layout, and even concepts as "soft" as creativity.

Coupled with this new sensing and data mining technology, the findings in this book can help us imagine what organizations could be. I'll take a quick tour through history to help you understand all the different ways people have organized themselves since humans first formed tribes millennia ago. Looking to the future, we can use this knowledge to create fundamentally new ways of organizing people that will radically improve the way we work. Office layouts that respond to social context and real-time feedback on communication patterns and interaction styles are new levers enabled by people analytics that no one could have imagined.

This book is by no means the final say on the topic of people analytics—rather, it is a beginning. The years ahead will offer many new opportunities for people analytics that cannot possibly be anticipated. The following pages explore some of those limitless possibilities, their foundations in history, and some paths to the future.

1

Sensible Organizations
Sensors, Big Data, and Quantifying the Unquantifiable

What if I told you that changing when you take a coffee break could make you more productive? Or that one of the biggest decisions a company makes revolves around the size of its lunch tables? These are things that traditional theory never looked at, indeed couldn't look at, because there was no way to measure them.

If people have learned anything over the past few decades, it's that using data to build organizations is better than following instinct. There is a reason the first "moneyball" team in major league baseball, the Oakland Athletics (in a now well-publicized example of data versus instinct) performed so well with a paltry budget: they used data to drive their decisions. Sidestepping convention, they relied on player metrics to assemble the best team possible within their budget, a strategy that resulted in a 20-game winning streak and a trip to the playoffs, even though they had the third-lowest payroll in the league.

Life is a game of small percentages. The difference in baseball between an average player and an all-star can be as small as a five-percentage point difference in batting average (between a 0.300 hitter and a 0.250 hitter, for example). If someone were able to develop a method to raise his individual performance by 5%, it would cause a tectonic shift in the way baseball players are evaluated.

The same is true in business. Research has shown that companies that use data to drive their business decisions perform 5% better than their peers.[1] Consider that large and diverse industries—from insurance companies to retail department stores—have profit margins of

1

less than 5%. A 5% performance increase in one of these companies would result in a profit roughly double that of its competitors.

As a result, many companies now try to use data-driven decision making throughout their operations. Probably the best example of this comes from big-box retailer Target.[2]

Target is a master at using analytics in their business. They have a dedicated statistics department whose sole purpose is to mine the mountains of data they've assembled across their stores to find new insights they can use to sell more products. This data isn't just a list of the things you've bought from Target. It's also demographic information: age, gender, marital status, number of children, home address, and so on. Even activity from their website is incorporated into customer models.

The big issue for Target is that in most cases our purchasing patterns don't change very much. We have a regular routine of going to the grocery store for food, going to the mall to buy clothes, and so on. Target, however, sells everything from electronics to food to furniture. They needed to change customers' habits so that when they think of buying any of those items, their first impulse is to head to Target.

Unfortunately for retailers, influencing someone's shopping behavior is incredibly difficult. These behaviors only change at a few key times throughout our lives, and other than that they are essentially locked in. These key times center on a few major events, such as moving to a new city or having a baby. From the data retailers collect, it's hard to predict if a customer is going to move. Maybe a customer buys some luggage or some bungee cords to strap it to his car, but even if that purchase indicates to retailers that the person is moving (which it probably doesn't), they still wouldn't know where the customer was moving. This means retailers can't give the person coupons to get him to come to their store, because they have no idea if the store is 1 mile or 100 miles away from his new home.

Instead, most retailers focus on the easier problem of predicting births, which means recognizing that a customer is pregnant. The reason Target in particular took this approach is that as soon as you have a kid, your mailbox is inundated with coupons from virtually every retailer within a 20-mile radius because birth records are public.

Retailers constantly poll those records and use them to send out mailings in the hopes that their coupon will be the one to bring you into their fold. Of course, with so many mailings the chance that a particular retailer will be picked is quite slim. Instead, retailers want to get ahead of the game. If Target could figure out, months before their competition, that you were going to have a child, they would be assured of a captive audience for their products.

So, Target's statistics department dove headfirst into this challenge. It was a relatively straightforward analytics problem, because the public birth records delivered hard data on what the statisticians were trying to predict. They found that analyzing purchases in 25 product categories provided extremely high predictive accuracy, with their algorithm's estimates coming very close to actual due dates. After developing this model, Target could then offer coupons throughout a woman's pregnancy that were targeted for her specific trimester (lots of vitamin supplements during the first trimester, for example), in addition to the all-important behavior-changing coupons that were sent right before the baby was due.

In fact, these models actually became *too* good. Some people, for various reasons, wanted to keep their pregnancy a secret. Target learned this lesson the hard way when their algorithm identified a particular individual as pregnant, triggering the flow of coupons to her house. Unfortunately, she was still in high school. After receiving the mailing, her father visited the local Target. He was not pleased.

"My daughter got this in the mail!" he said. "She's still in high school, and you're sending her coupons for baby clothes and cribs? Are you trying to encourage her to get pregnant?"

The manager apologized and was able to defuse the situation. He even called the father a few days later to apologize again. The father, however, had a quite different tone this time around.

"I had a talk with my daughter," he said. "It turns out there's been some activities in my house I haven't been completely aware of. She's due in August. I owe you an apology."

The algorithm Target had developed was so good that it could recognize pregnancy even better than a family member who saw that girl *every day*. This is the power of analytics—providing a nearly superhuman ability to understand and change the world around us.

Although these analytics aren't perfect, they are orders of magnitude more effective than the overly simplistic methods of the past. This is why so many companies, from Target to Netflix to Amazon, make analytics a central part of their corporate strategy.

This data-driven approach, however, isn't regularly applied *inside* companies. There just hasn't been a good way to measure how people actually work. Surveys and interviews are fall-back approaches, but they become invalid and fantastically inaccurate in a wide variety of circumstances—for example, when an employee has a bad day, forgets something, has just eaten lunch, and so on.

The beauty of Target's approach is that they used data on behavior (in this case, purchasing decisions) to make predictions. To extend this approach to the workplace, you need data on how people are actually behaving. As Target showed, digging into this real-world data can open up amazing opportunities.

Telescopes, Microscopes, and "Socioscopes"

New data can fundamentally change the way people view the world. When we look at the world through any particular lens, we are bound to create theories that deal with reality at that level of detail. When our ancestors saw points of light in the sky, they assumed that they existed as points of light orbiting above on a complex set of spheres. When they were able to look through a telescope and see that in fact some of those points of light appear larger and even have other celestial bodies orbiting them, they had to reconsider their model of reality.

New methods of observation have systematically reinvented fields across the scientific landscape; for example, the telescope revolutionized the study of astronomy, and the microscope revolutionized the study of biology and chemistry. However, social science has never experienced a revolution of this sort. Researchers still use pen and paper surveys, human observers, and laboratory confederates to attempt to untangle the myriad phenomena that constitute our society.

The lack of effective measurement tools isn't unique to social science. Nearly every scientific field has at some point dealt with a paucity of data. Astronomy is a great example. For millions of years people looked up at the sky to observe the stars, but there was astoundingly little hard data on celestial movement until only a few hundred years ago. The primary issue was that people who actually wrote down their observations would only do so for short periods of time, using dead reckoning to estimate the movement of the stars.

As astronomers tried to develop models to explain celestial movement, the lack of data meant that testing any model was essentially impossible. Traditional astronomical models always broke down because of the phenomenon of apparent retrograde motion—the appearance of some stars (actually the planets in our solar system) moving in one direction on some nights only to switch direction in following nights. Today, we know that this is because all planets orbit the sun, and because each planet orbits the sun at different speeds they can appear from Earth as if they change direction.

Aristotle created a model that seemed to fit with these observations: one with the Earth at the center of the universe and with stars arrayed on a series of circular "celestial spheres" that spun around our planet. It took almost 2,000 years for an alternative model to be proposed. Interestingly, it was data, not the relative simplicity of these new models, that changed our view of the universe.

Brahe and Kepler

In the mid-sixteenth century, Copernicus had unveiled his new theory of planetary motion, placing the sun at the center of our solar system. This was a drastic change from the previous model which had Earth at the center, but this theory found little acceptance because his hypothesized circular orbits didn't fit the reality of elliptical orbits.

Soon after this, a Danish nobleman named Tycho Brahe took it upon himself to assemble the most complete astronomical record in history. Tycho spent years of his life in a custom-built observatory that allowed his assistants to record his nightly observations of stellar and planetary positions. This massive compendium provided Johannes Kepler, one of Tycho's assistants, with a dataset that allowed him to clearly show an elliptical orbit around the sun. Kepler's model demonstrated unprecedented accuracy in predicting the movement of celestial bodies, which led to broad acceptance of the heliocentric model.

It's no coincidence that Kepler's model emerged directly from Tycho's observations. Earlier astronomical observations had been limited to sparse records from a smattering of individuals in different parts of the world at different times, and never in an observatory that allowed for much more than educated guessing.

These problems are similar to the ones that social scientists are grappling with today: Studies are qualitative, observational, and limited to small pockets of what individual researchers can directly observe. Many researchers point to the rigorous training that they go through before making those observations as evidence of the strength of social science research. However, this argument merely ignores the problems that confront the advancement of work in this field.

Unbiased?

Social science has given organizations some powerful tools over the last century. Its findings have become cornerstones in much of the world of work, from product development to organizational design. Social science measurement tools, however, were initially devised decades ago. Surveys, human observers, aptitude tests, and controlled laboratory experiments are the tools of the social science trade. While certainly useful, each of these tools has some fundamental weaknesses.

Everyone is familiar with surveys, and you've probably been asked countless times by store employees to fill out an online survey about your experience. How often do you actually fill out those surveys— once a month, once a year, never? Maybe only people thrilled with their experience answer the survey. Maybe only people who had a terrible experience or people who just feel a sense of responsibility to answer respond. This sample is clearly biased, because stores are only getting data from a small fraction of their customers, and the vast majority of typical experiences are left out. However, even responses from typical consumers can be biased. If you had a bad day, your answers tend to be more negative. If it's a beautiful day outside, your responses are more positive.

Researchers try to correct this bias problem by using observational data. Highly trained ethnographers and anthropologists integrate themselves into an environment and collect unbiased data on the activity they observe. This method runs into two major issues: individual differences and scale.

Different observers naturally see different things. Even with thousands of hours of training, observers can differ in something as simple as classifying what constitutes a conversation. On top of this challenge, having more than a few observers in one environment at the same time is impractical, so anyone trying to understand the behavior of thousands or millions of individuals would be out of luck.

Until recently, this methodological approach was essentially the end of the story. Simply no tool existed that would enable the understanding of human behavior on a massive scale at any fine-grained level of detail. Ironically, a revolution in social science data collection didn't come from a desire to collect data. It came from a new communication tool: e-mail.

Digital Breadcrumbs

We all leave vast traces of digital breadcrumbs on our computers: contents of documents, program usage, and most notably the information sent to other people through e-mail messages. This is a treasure trove of information for researchers, because it essentially composes a log of a person's activity throughout the day. Accessing most of this information would require a program to be installed on each individual's computer, constantly logging every keystroke and program action and uploading this information to a server.

E-mail is different. When you send an e-mail from Gmail, for example, your message first goes to Google's outgoing e-mail server, which then sends it on its way across the Internet. This activity is logged by the server and is how Google is able to save your e-mail in your Sent folder. When you receive an e-mail, it is also first logged on

Google's servers before you even see it. In most e-mail setups, messages remain on the server even after you download them.

Think about what this information represents: a digital contact list that contains information on everyone with whom you've ever communicated, and even information on what you communicated about. Researchers have recently begun to capitalize on this data and show its true value. For now, suffice it to say that because people frequently collaborate using electronic communication technologies, analyzing this e-mail data is critical for understanding how organizations really work.

"Socioscope"

Electronic records have only one flaw: They are completely disconnected from reality. The people whom you talk to and spend time with are not necessarily the people you e-mail. Most important events happen in the real world. Corporate mergers don't happen through IMs (instant messages). People don't take coffee breaks with colleagues a continent away. These moments are central to everyone's daily lives, and they are completely absent in digital breadcrumbs.

Soon after the advent of e-mail, however, a technological explosion of a different kind enabled a similar lens into the real world: the massive proliferation of sensors.

When most people think of sensors, they imagine being strapped into an EEG with electrodes attached to their head, or full body suits with cumbersome helmets that track every movement. What they often forget is that everyone already carries around dozens of sensors every day.

Most people carry some ID cards in their wallet. Regardless of whether the cards were issued by a company or school, most modern ID cards have an embedded RFID (radio frequency identification) chip. This chip allows people to tap their card onto a reader to open a door. This same sensor could also be used to track a person's location by placing RFID readers throughout an office. The readers would constantly send out requests for the RFID card to send its ID, and by observing which reader detected the card, a computer could recognize where the person was located.

In sensing terms, this RFID device is very simple. It has just one radio, and it provides a rough estimate of location. What if you augmented this ID card with some additional sensors? What things could you learn?

Infra-red (IR) Devices

In the mid-1990s, scientists began to experiment with sensing devices to answer these questions. Most of these applications focused on enabling people to keep a personal record of whom they interacted with at large events such as conferences or company meetings. This tracking was accomplished mainly by using a basic infra-red (IR) transceiver to recognize when two people were facing each other.

An IR transceiver is a common device that functions in essentially the same way as a TV remote control. If one person wearing an IR transceiver faces another person wearing the same device, a detection registers. Seeing enough of these detections indicates that two people are likely talking to each other (mostly because standing and facing someone for a few minutes and not at least saying hello would be awkward).

Accelerometers

Other scientists used ID badges in the medical field. Instead of IR transceivers, they added an accelerometer (a motion sensor) to the traditional RFID badge to look at how the movement of people changed over time. For example, research with accelerometers has been used to study people with degenerative diseases, such as Parkinson's or ALS (Lou Gehrig's disease). These diseases cause physical tremors and a decline in motor function. Data from an accelerometer allows for precise measurement of disease progression and can gauge the effectiveness of different treatments.

Different accelerometers work in different ways, but the general idea is that they have a chip with three microscopic weights inside, one for each of the three spatial dimensions (x, y, z). Acceleration causes the weights to shift, and the degree to which they shift indicates how fast you're accelerating. If you've heard of an accelerometer before, it's probably because it's the same sensor that the iPhone and other devices use to let you interact with the device by moving it around. The accelerometer tells your phone that it's been tipped on its side, shifting the screen to a landscape view.

Microphones

Microphones have also been added to ID badges, especially in the medical field. Vocera Communication's communicator allows physicians to talk immediately to other medical staff using voice dialing phrases or names, especially helpful in situations where knowing where other people are can be difficult. Of course, microphones can also be used to record what people say, but more recently scientists have used microphones to analyze sound in real time. Researchers from Dartmouth used audio data from cellphone microphones to recognize everyday locations, such as cafeterias, offices, or the inside of your car. The idea is to listen for unique sounds, such as the clattering of plates or the click of a car's turn signal, to determine where a person is.

Sociometer

In the early 2000s, researchers at MIT's Human Dynamics group began combining multiple sensors into a single device. The idea was to make a general ID badge that would be able to measure all the different signals—IR, motion, and sound—at the same time. This kind of badge could do things that no device had been able to do before. For example, if you want to know exactly when two people are talking to each other, you really need an IR transceiver, a microphone, and a proximity sensor.

This general-purpose sensing device became known as the *Sociometer*. Originally, it contained only an IR transceiver, microphone, and two accelerometers. The Sociometer was essentially a gray box the size of a paperback book strapped across your chest—needless to say, not something you would want to wear through airport security. Despite its shortcomings in form factor, this device was the first of its kind—one system that incorporated the critical sensors necessary to understand many aspects of human behavior. As with most prototype devices, using it outside of tightly controlled settings was difficult. Initial experiments took place in the lab and then transitioned to limited field trials within MIT. Sandy Pentland's book *Honest Signals* describes these experiments in great detail, but I summarize the most relevant ones in this chapter.

Predicting Speed-Dating Outcomes

Researchers at MIT initially used the audio processing technology of the Sociometer platform to examine behavior in controlled environments to demonstrate the future potential of this technology. A microphone recorded high-quality audio so that researchers could determine what aspects of speech are most important when trying to predict different outcomes.

Perhaps stereotypically for nerdy engineering types, the MIT researchers studied a situation that was most challenging to them: dating. Knowing the right words to say doesn't guarantee a date with someone; rather, the mood and the chemistry between people are important. Can these things be quantified?

Researchers took these sensors to local speed-dating events to answer that very question. For those who aren't familiar with the concept, speed dating operates on the principle that after five minutes people know whether they're compatible. Central to a speed-dating event is the seating arrangement. Women sit at tables arranged in rows, and men rotate from table to table every five minutes. At the end of the event, the romantic hopefuls check off boxes to indicate who they would like to go out with on a date and hand these slips to the organizers. When there is a match, the organizers send both people an e-mail with their date's contact information.

In this experiment researchers recorded dozens of these five-minute interactions and attempted to predict whether people would choose to go out on a date. Researchers didn't look at the content of the conversation, only *how* people were talking—their "social signals."

Social signals are the unconscious messages that people pass to one another when they're talking. Things as subtle as a slight change in tone, an interruption, or a raised eyebrow are all social signals that convey important information beyond the content of conversations. Using complex algorithms, researchers were able to automatically calculate the tone of voice, changes in speaking volume, and speaking speed of study participants. It turns out that with only these features, not looking at any content, the researchers were able to predict who would go on a date with about 85% accuracy. Incidentally, it turned out that only the woman's voice features were predictive, probably because the men seemed to be interested in everyone—perhaps not the most startling discovery, but one for which we now have scientific backing.

These results were encouraging because they surpassed the state of the art in behavioral measurement up to that point, which mostly consisted of researchers' painstakingly coding recorded audio by hand. At the time, however, it was unclear if the experiment result was an aberration or representative of the power of this method of data analysis. Also, although speed dating is of interest to many people, it's somewhat separated from the larger impact that researchers envisioned for this technology. So they turned their attention to something that's of vital economic importance: salary negotiation.

Negotiations Broken Down

In general, salary negotiation is difficult to navigate effectively. From a simplified viewpoint, employers want to pay the lowest amount possible but keep prospective employees from walking away, while employees want to maximize their salary while keeping the employer from balking at a ridiculous wage.

Traditional theory holds that the most important advantage in a negotiation is information. For example, if you're an employer who wants an employee to start on June 1 and you learn that she wants to start on June 1 as well, you have an advantage. You can say you want her to start on a different date, and then "concede" that she can start on June 1, but she'll have to give up some of her signing bonus.

This theory vastly discounts the effects of social signals. A dominant individual with the same information should reach roughly the same outcome as a shier person. Non-theoretical experience, of course, would dictate otherwise, and this study set out to examine precisely this issue.

To control as many variables as possible, researchers at MIT set up a laboratory study on salary negotiations. The experiment duplicated what you would see at most companies across America. A job candidate meets with a recruiter to negotiate a compensation package, with eight key areas on the table: starting date, salary, job assignment, company car, signing bonus, vacation days, moving expense reimbursement, and insurance provider. For each area, the researchers assigned participants a specific target number as well as a number of points for different outcomes. For example, a candidate who got a 10% signing bonus would receive 4,000 points while the recruiter would receive 0 points. On the other hand, a 2% bonus would translate into 0 points for the candidate and 1,600 points for the recruiter. Participants saw only their own points schedule; and if they came to an agreement, participants were paid at the end of the study based on the number of points they received.

When the participants sat down to the table, they turned on a small recording device. Researchers automatically extracted social signals from this audio data so they could study the data's predictive power. They even raised the stakes. These negotiations typically went on for about 40 minutes, but researchers wanted to test whether the conversational style at the beginning of the negotiation would predict the results at the end. Astoundingly, the social signals (in this case, specifically modulation in volume and speaking rate) from the first 5 minutes were responsible for about 30% of the final salary.

This result was another powerful illustration of the importance of these social signals and the ability of wearable sensors to capture them. To get a sense for the magnitude of this result, this research indicates that if you are looking for an entry-level software engineer position, just changing the way you talk to your prospective employer would give you a 30% greater chance of pulling in $90,000 versus $65,000.

Overcoming the instinctive belief that the content of the conversation is what matters most can be difficult. Certainly, if President Obama delivered a speech expounding on last night's episode of *Survivor* instead of one on health-care reform, the public would be puzzled to say the least. However, as long as people stay on topic, the non-content cues are influential.

A great illustration of the impact of social signals is how people can appreciate foreign language films. Imagine that you're watching a film in another language and you turn off the subtitles. You can't understand what they're talking about, but you get the sense from their tone of voice, posture, and gestures that one character doesn't like another, or that these people are having a heated discussion. The signals you're paying attention to are exactly the same ones that these sensors are measuring.

Overall, the results from these initial studies were considered astonishing. A computer and a few clever algorithms had managed to predict the outcome of complex situations with startling accuracy, previously thought to be solely the province of human beings. Overstating how important these findings were is difficult. *For the first time, human behavior could be objectively measured outside of the laboratory.*

Enter the Badge

This leap forward in measurement technology embodied in the Sociometer platform enabled researchers to ask fundamentally new questions about how people work: Do bosses dominate conversations with their subordinates? What does corporate culture really mean? Scale and level of detail ceased to be limiting factors when observing behavior.

With this new technology, data collection is no longer the bottleneck for social science. Within a few months of deploying Sociometers and their technological descendants, researchers collected more data than had been assembled throughout centuries of observational methods. Instead, the limiting factor for sensor-based data collection became technology adoption.

The original Sociometer was heavy and awkward to wear. The Sociometer also didn't provide study participants with any direct benefit beyond the general social good they would accrue for contributing to the advancement of science. It would also be months before they could receive feedback on their own behavior. Combined, these drawbacks put a heavy burden on participants, and made it difficult to envision widespread acceptance of this technology.

To combat these drawbacks, researchers integrated display functionality into the next version of the Sociometer system, dubbed the UberBadge. The UberBadge vastly improved the form factor of the Sociometer, taking the same sensing devices and packing them into a badge the size of a wide wallet. The badge also included an LED display on the front, allowing researchers to display scrolling messages. This helped users get some benefit out of the badges—such as displaying the length of a conversation or how many people they met at an event—and being able to wear it around the neck made them much easier to use.

By changing the way people wore the badges, researchers had found an avenue to broad adoption. However, with these early sensing devices, privacy was a major concern. These badges collected the actual content of conversations. It's safe to say that most people don't want to wear a device that records everything they say. It's also against the law in most states.

The rapid reduction in sensor size and power consumption, as well as gains in battery life, provided the solution to this privacy problem. With extra power, future versions of the badge could process audio data in real time, recording only *features* of conversations—volume, pitch, and emphasis—a few times a second instead of the *content*.

This newest device, the Sociometric Badge, is the size of a deck of cards and weighs about as much as five U.S. quarters (see Figure 1.1). The badge incorporates all the sensors of the previous devices: a microphone, IR transceiver, and accelerometer—and has the addition of a Bluetooth radio. The badge can collect data continuously for about 40 hours, or one work week, without needing to be recharged. With the data analysis algorithms built into the badge, it could save the equivalent of one work year of behavioral data onto a 4GB SD card.

Figure 1.1 The Sociometric Badge

You can think of the Sociometric Badge as the natural evolution of the company ID badge. No longer just a tool to open doors, this new kind of ID badge enables you to understand yourself and your company at large through data-driven reports and feedback. As shown from the examples in this chapter, this sensor technology has amazing potential. From gathering five minutes of data with the badge, you could figure out not only whether you'll win a negotiation, but how well you'll do. With this badge deployed across millions of individuals at different companies in countries all over the world for not minutes but years or decades, imagine what we could learn about to help people collaborate more effectively and create better organizations.

The opportunities offered by using the badge technology not only can revolutionize our understanding of organizations and society at large, but can also be used to create organizations where privacy is a thing of the past, and managers watch every movement, every conversation, looking for inefficiencies. Ironically, this means that data abundance, rather than scarcity, becomes the biggest hurdle to overcome.

Big Data = Big Brother?

Sensing data can be a major threat to privacy. Whether the data is from cellphones or web browsing histories, the potential abuse of this massive trove of data is an important concern. At the same time, awareness of this issue is alarmingly low, which means that people often don't understand the power of the data that they make available.

This problem is magnified with the Sociometric Badge. Companies can already legally

- Watch employees via CCTV
- Log keystrokes
- Take screenshots of employees using their company computers
- Read employee e-mails

Exposing additional sensitive information from the badges, such as location and who you talked to, could lead to egregious abuses. This data could allow companies to determine when you're in the bathroom, how much time you "wasted" talking to your friend in another department, and so on. Under current U.S. law, this kind of monitoring is completely legal.

This is a major failing of the U.S. legal system. Overreaching corporate monitoring should not only be morally distasteful, it should also be illegal. Most countries in Europe and Asia ban this activity, but they go so far as to prevent most analysis of this kind of data. To reach a productive middle ground, individuals and companies need to agree on steps to take when dealing with this extremely sensitive data.

The projects described in this book adhere to the "new deal on data" championed by MIT Professor Sandy Pentland. The core concepts of this new deal boil down to these three points:

- Data collection is opt-in and uses informed consent.
- Individuals control their own data.
- Any data sent to third parties must be aggregated.

The following sections examine each of these rules individually to help you understand why they're necessary for reasonable application of sensing technology and "big data" analytics in general.

Opt-In

As mentioned previously, companies already collect a lot of data without your *informed* consent. For example, when the organizations I've been part of collect data with the Sociometric Badge, we spend weeks answering questions from participants, explaining what data we collect, and even give them consent forms that have our actual database tables. If people don't want to participate, we also hand out "fake" badges that don't collect data but otherwise look and act just like normal badges. This prevents those uncomfortable with the technology from being singled out, and in general makes everyone more likely to participate. Participants can also opt-out at any time. In practice this happens very rarely, because after a few days' time people essentially forget that they're wearing the badges.

Taken together, these steps help assuage people's concerns and help us consistently achieve more than a 90% participation rate in all of our projects. Compare that to surveys, where researchers are ecstatic to get a 50% response rate.

With such high participation rates, the data itself becomes even more valuable; and whenever something is that important, everyone is going to try to stake their claim to it.

Data Control

Modern companies are extremely protective of their data—as they should be. Google's entire revenue stream, for example, is dependent on the data created by its users. This protectiveness extends to corporate e-mail, where courts have continually reaffirmed the rights of companies to read their employees' e-mails as long as they are accessed through company servers.

The sensitive nature of Sociometric Badge data points to the necessity of a change in this model. Without individual control of data, companies would be free to use your data any way they saw fit. For example, this kind of data could predict health risks (depression can be predicted from changes in communication patterns) or your likelihood to leave the organization (people getting ready to quit start to withdraw socially before making the announcement), leading your superiors to pass you over for promotion or diminish your role. If individuals control their own data, then any potential abuse can immediately be avoided by individuals denying access to their data. In the case of the projects described in this book, individuals can delete their data at will to prevent access to their information.

Overall, there generally are no good business reasons for companies to control the data of individuals. Knowing where Bob is at 2:30 on Tuesday, for example, doesn't tell you about productivity. Companies should care much more about the general patterns and aggregate statistics that describe how different teams and divisions are collaborating and what behaviors and interaction patterns make people happy and effective. These aggregate statistics are also the only way to preserve privacy.

Data Aggregation

Anonymizing data from sensors is essentially impossible. Mathematically, it's incredibly unlikely that someone would go to the exact same places and talk to the same people as you. Even if someone took a notebook and simply wrote down some of the times that a target person talked to others, then that someone would know whether he had the target's sensor data.

The only way to deal with this problem is to aggregate data. Instead of allowing everyone to see information about each individual, the data is averaged over groups. This allows people to compare different teams and see how their own behavior stacks up in their group, but prevents anyone from identifying a specific person.

In my experience, companies usually aren't too concerned by this restriction. People still get their individual data and can use it to improve. For example, they could see that they're not interacting enough with another team on a project, or that compared to the happiest people at their company they tend to go to the coffee machine less frequently. The organization sees the aggregate data and general trends, which it can use to identify behaviors and collaboration patterns that make people and teams happier and more effective. This approach gives everyone what they want, even reducing liability for companies in case their servers get hacked. Because they don't have individual data, even someone with malicious intentions couldn't use the data to discriminate or spy on a coworker or employee.

To a lesser extent, companies today actually struggle with data anonymization problems. How does an organization deal with salary information? What happens if you submit a complaint about a coworker? Creating an organization that is open in its approach to these questions is critical not only for gaining widespread acceptance for this technology, but also for building a successful organization.

Trust and Transparency

At the core of the precepts outlined in this chapter are the importance of trust and transparency in organizations. If you don't trust the people you work with and work for, you're going to be unhappy, unproductive, and generally looking to jump ship for another job as soon as you can. If organizations instead position data collection policies to increase trust and transparency, employees learn how to improve and be happier, and companies can vastly increase their success.

People also shouldn't be overly distracted by the privacy concerns associated with the widespread adoption of sensing technologies. As discussed in the coming pages, this technology has the potential to bring about radical, positive change in the way people work, from changing what it means to have an org chart to making management focus on people first. Ethically applying this technology and realizing these amazing possibilities is up to us.

In reality, however, the things that actually make people effective at work aren't new. They have ancient origins, millions of years in the making. Even the concept of an organization has roots that stretch back for millennia.

Before we start looking at where we're going, in the next chapter we'll take a look at where we've been.

2

Evolution, History, and Social Behavior
Our Wandering Road to the Modern Corporation

In his seminal novel *I, Robot,* Isaac Asimov spun tales of a future where humanoid robots were an integral part of our society. They cared for, worked with, and were controlled by humans. Robots had many different functions, but they all had one thing in common: the three laws of robotics.

These laws were designed to protect the robots' human creators:

- A robot may not injure a human being or, through inaction, allow a human being to come to harm.
- A robot must obey the orders given to it by human beings, except where such orders would conflict with the First Law.
- A robot must protect its own existence as long as such protection does not conflict with the First or Second Laws.

Supposedly every other aspect of robot behavior was governed by their individual programming as long as it complied with the three laws.

However people noticed that robots had some other process guiding their behaviors. Muses one of the story's protagonists in the film adaptation:

Why is it that when robots are stored in an empty space, they will group together rather than stand alone?

One could ask the same question of humanity. Why is it that two people in an empty room talk to each other rather than stare mutely at the floor? Why is it that we choose to work together rather than to work separately? Are these behaviors learned in our recent history, or are they something deeper, something more fundamental about being human?

Although there are certainly some general rules governing our behavior, fortunately or unfortunately we don't have anything like the three laws of robotics to help people make sense of human groups. We need a basic understanding of how people evolved biologically and culturally to work together in order to uncover general principles around how people collaborate. These patterns will help identify what aspects of behavior are really important for collaboration and what data will be useful for analyzing today's organizations.

Back to the Future

Since our pre-human ancestors climbed into the trees, we've been working in groups. Even for these ancestors, groups provided some fundamental advantages over individual action, the most obvious one being that you can better defend yourself when you're part of a group. Simply more fists and weapons are available when you're with others. You can also spread risk across many individuals in a group. When foraging for food, for example, your individual probability of success is fairly low. If you're in a group that shares its food, however, even if you're mostly unsuccessful, you'll still be able to survive. Lastly, you can do bigger things when you're in a bigger group. It might take three individuals to lift a rock that obscures a treasure trove of ants or other insects. Looking at our pre-human, chimp-like ancestors, then, seems like a perfect place to start in our investigation into the history of groups.

In the Shadow of Man

Let's turn back the clock about three million years. Humans, homo sapiens, didn't exist. In fact, most species that we know today didn't exist. Our evolutionary ancestors of that time looked a lot like chimpanzees, from their sloping foreheads to their diminutive size. While fossil records are fuzzy at best, our ancestors come from one of the species from the genus *Australopithecus*, a group of short bipeds that could nearly chew through rock. Intellectually, however, their relatively small brains indicate that they were cognitively on par with modern gorillas and chimpanzees.

Our ancestors spent most of their days foraging, hiding from predators, and sleeping. Importantly, they were also able to stand upright. This one difference is believed to be one of the main reasons for our ancestors' success, because it allowed them to walk and use tools at the same time.

We also know that these ancestors lived in groups. Considerable debate still exists about exactly how large the groups were and how they behaved. We really only have fossils to go on. Luckily, present-day analogues can provide some insight: gorillas, bonobos, and chimpanzees.

Gorillas

Most of us have seen gorillas in the zoo or on one of the many nature programs that populate the Discovery Channel. Despite their massive size, these ground-dwelling behemoths are primarily herbivores. Their large gut enables them to wolf down anything from fruit to pith, the woody stems of some plants.

Because their diet can accommodate most available food sources, gorillas don't have to spend a lot of their time foraging. Gorillas typically travel around an area not more than a few miles in diameter, and on any given day they move less than a third of a mile. In contrast, the average human walks about five miles in a day.

Mountain gorillas typically live in small "troops" of 5 to 30 gorillas. As a group has to cover more distance to forage, smaller groups will gradually get larger. This is a direct result of the risk mitigation property of troops, because with more gorillas they can discover rich food sources more effectively. After a certain point, however, adding more gorillas to a troop has little effect on foraging efficiency.[1]

To understand that phenomenon, just examine the foraging process. Gorillas start off from a central point, going off in different directions in search of food. If they go more than a third of a mile without finding anything, then they'll turn back. If there are too many gorillas, however, then this search becomes redundant. Different gorillas will be covering the same ground.

Gorillas could theoretically walk longer distances to find more food. However, the extra walking would increase a troop's calorie expenditure, meaning that splitting into different groups would be more effective. In summary, for gorillas some benefit exists to being in a group, but after a group gets too big, those benefits decline.

Although gorilla and human societies are clearly not the same, their traits give us clues about how our ancestors might have lived and worked.

For us what's interesting is that gorilla groups are most effective when they are relatively large, but not too large. There are simply no extremely large groups in gorilla societies, and this likely held for our ancestors as well. This evidence is also supported by some of our other ape relatives, such as bonobos.

Bonobos

Bonobos (*Pan paniscus*) are one of our closest relatives in the animal kingdom, with our last common ancestor living some 6 million years ago. Also called the pygmy chimpanzee, bonobos probably separated from the common chimpanzee around 1.5 million years ago.

Bonobos contrast strongly with gorillas. They are much smaller, can form larger groups, and range over areas as large as 16 miles. This is necessary because they can't eat as wide a variety of food as gorillas, and so depend on high-calorie foods such as fruit and meat to survive.

Bonobo society is actually quite similar to that of humans. They form large groups, sometimes more than 100 members, but they can forage in smaller parties of only 6 or 7 bonobos.[2] These smaller parties often split off for days at a time, but they always come back to the larger group. This is a nice way to reap the benefits of large communities without exhausting the local food supply.

The local environment dictates how often this splitting occurs. When fruit is plentiful, bonobos stick together in one large group. There's no need for them to go their separate ways scouring the area for fruit without the inherent protection of the larger group. When food is rare, small parties fan out across a wide area to explore and report any discoveries to the group. These foraging parties typically stay constant over time, but they're not necessarily formed along familial lines. These small, cohesive foraging parties are essentially the core of bonobo social life. Interestingly, the society of their close genetic relative, chimpanzees, looks very different.

Common Chimpanzees

Common chimpanzees are physiologically very similar to bonobos, separated by only 1.5 million years of evolutionary history. Chimpanzees also form larger social groups, and have wide home ranges of up to 40 miles. These groups can range from 20 to more than 150 individuals, although typically they are in the lower part of that range.

Compared to bonobos, chimps live in an environment where access to food is much less certain. They can still break up into smaller foraging parties, but they have to cooperate with the larger group to survive. Although starvation isn't a frequent occurrence in chimp societies, the dominance hierarchy is crucial in determining who gets food first, and therefore who is able to reproduce more easily.

Chimpanzees are also proficient hunters. They form complex hunting groups where different chimps take on different roles, constructing a sophisticated strategy for cornering small game. Some chimpanzees are assigned as chasers, who pursue the quarry. Blockers corral the prey until they reach the hiding ambushers, who catch and kill the animal. Importantly, food is shared not just among the hunting group but also with other nearby chimps.

This is a complicated activity, especially considering that chimpanzees aren't able to communicate with a higher order language. They need to be able to understand this strategy, to plan and execute and change their plans on the fly. We typically associate these activities only with humans and with language, but clearly our ancestors must have engaged in these activities as well.

Importantly, however, a hard cap exists on group size for all apes. You simply don't see apes in groups that are much greater than 150 individuals. Significantly, this is basically the same as the cap for humans, what is known as the *Dunbar number*.

The Dunbar number is the upper limit on the number of people a human being can know "well." This concept was developed by the British anthropologist Robin Dunbar, who surveyed groups across human history and found that the most cohesive unit of coordination peaked at about 150 people. Small villages and military units had this common upper bound beyond which cohesion and performance started to break down.

Humans can naturally have larger groups, and some have put the Dunbar number as high as 230. Nevertheless, it is not an order of magnitude above the group size for chimpanzees. Rather we can see a steady change from our common ancestor to humanity's current state.

Somewhere along the way, these groups became organizations, but finding an exact point in time when this occurred is difficult. Is there a significant difference between humans roaming the plains hunting large game and chimpanzees hunting animals in the forest? Suffice it to say that sometime within the last thousand years people began living in large enough groups to form cities, and it was during that time that a group that could be considered sufficiently close to an "organization" was formed.

You Say "Groups," I Say "Organizations"

The definition of an "organization" is somewhat arbitrary—it has both similarities with and differences from a group. An organization is not simply a collection (or group) of people, such as everybody under the age of 25 or everyone who lives in an apartment building above the fifth floor. Clearly, when you think of an organization, the idea is that the people inside the organization are more connected to each other than one would expect by chance. In addition, this collection of individuals has to have a set of formal and informal processes that govern the behavior of the organization's members. This distinguishes organizations as a subcategory of groups. In other words, all organizations are groups, but not all groups are organizations.

By this definition your group of friends is not an organization. They have no formal mechanisms for collective action. Although there will be informal consequences if one of your friends offends you, these rules aren't written down anywhere. If they are, this is much more like a secret club, and you should seriously reconsider your choice of companions.

Of course, gray areas exist. Especially with the explosion of online communities, the boundary between groups and organizations has started to blur. As Tom Malone argues in *The Future of Work*, some of these online communities are most assuredly organizations. In his later work he singles out guilds in the *World of Warcraft* (WoW) as a prime example of what a modern organization can be.

For the uninitiated, the WoW is a Massively Multiplayer Online Role-Playing Game (or MMORPG. Say that ten times fast). In WoW, players from across the world create an online persona that battles virtual enemies to increase their power and in-game money. This is primarily accomplished through quests, where you venture out for hours to eventually face a powerful enemy. Should you triumph, you are rewarded with valuable loot in the form of armor, weapons, and other virtual riches. As your character gets more powerful, these quests become increasingly difficult, to the point where you can't complete a quest by yourself.

This is where the WoW guilds come in. In most of these quests, the prize at the end is indivisible. That is, there is only one prize and only one member of the party can claim it. Guilds create a formal structure around this process, where loot is parceled out quest by quest to the different guild members who participate, ensuring that everyone gets his or her fair share. Guild members have to coordinate effectively to complete these difficult quests, and their online activity as well as the reward process is highly structured.

This certainly clashes with our modern notion of an organization: people sitting in an office in two-piece suits filing form after form. However, when you strip away the outer layers, WoW guilds look pretty similar to other organizations.

The Linux development community is a similar example. Linux is a completely open source operating system, one of the chief competitors to the juggernaut of this space, Microsoft Windows. Whereas

Microsoft develops Windows internally through its staff of programmers and engineers, Linux is developed by a worldwide community of people who aren't paid for their effort. Although some formal processes are in place for Linux development—to be added to the core system code, one has to undergo a rigorous screening process—the notion of "employees" doesn't exist here. It is an organization, but definitely a non-traditional one.

The distinction further blurs when you look at other online communities, such as the community of eBay merchants. These merchants rely on each other for accurate ratings of buyers and sellers in order to conduct their business. Merchants who violate customer trust need to be punished by the community. Otherwise, they risk diminishing the value of ratings for all sellers, driving buyers from the site. Although one might consider the rating system a formal process, the consequences of this system are harder to define. Still, these sellers need to create a vibrant marketplace to attract buyers, and they rely on each other for selling tips and policing scammers. Is this an organization? It's certainly unclear.

Families are also difficult from a classification perspective. Although families live together and help each other informally, legal processes and protocols also exist around the definition of a family. If family members criminally abuse each other, a formal punishment is applied. Despite these conventional aspects of a family group, defining "family" as an organization is difficult.

All of these examples are to make the point that organizations don't all look or act alike. Similar to our biological and cultural socialization mechanisms, organizations evolved over time, and there's not a clear point that can be identified as the birth of the organization.

Individual < Tribe < City-State

Organizations are needed because they offer some fundamental advantages over more informal means of association. To get a sense of these advantages, look back at the ape troops discussed earlier. They are definitely groups, and although they have complex social hierarchies, there are no formal processes to speak of. Early humans lived in similar groups as well. Hunting in tribes that were made up of close relatives and families, technological innovation (that is, tool development) occurred at the pace of roughly one discovery every 10,000 years until about 8,000 BC.

This rate of discovery is essentially at a chance level because hundreds of generations were using tools with little improvement. As the human population increased, the chances simply became more likely that someone would think up a new tool. But something happened around 10,000 years ago. Humans started living together in groups that became too large to manage through informal means. For the first time in history, humans had crossed the Dunbar number. Codes of conduct had to be recorded, and rules had to be agreed upon. In short, people needed a government.

The concept of a government was a radical shift from the informal mechanisms which had dominated up to that time. From the first organisms to form in Earth's oceans billions of years ago, life had developed on informal terms. Groups of animals would herd and act collectively, but these actions were heavily rooted in biological responses, honed through eons of evolutionary development. With the rise of civilization, humans realized the need for order to support our burgeoning aspirations.

Civilizations started out on a modest scale, with around 10,000 people living in early city-states. These city-states were foci of economic and agricultural activity, but tended to be fairly unstable. Smaller city-states would be subject to assault from larger neighbors, and, in fact, the first larger civilizations, such as Phoenicia and Babylon, were composed of a number of these city-states.

With so many people together in one place, city-states became places for the exchange of both goods and ideas, and this led to a much more rapid period of innovation. New technologies were emerging every hundred years or so, an order of magnitude faster than before. Recent work by Wei Pan and his colleagues at MIT have shown that the rate of innovation in cities is directly related to population density, which provides a clue as to why these early civilizations were so successful. They could create better technology, train better soldiers, and spread this influence to other affiliated city-states.

For city-states to run, however, they needed a number of basic services: roads, sanitation, and easily interpretable laws. The degree to which early societies were able to fulfill these needs had a direct impact on their success. The dominant civilization of the early historical era, Rome, provides a clear example of this relationship.

Do as the Romans Do

Like Greece before it, ancient Rome was a historical juggernaut. The Romans had scientific prowess that was second to none, delivering innovations such as concrete, the aqueduct, and indoor plumbing. Their army laid waste to their contemporary rivals, such as Carthage, the Gallic tribes, and the Kingdom of Pontus. From humble beginnings in 800 BC, Rome blossomed into a massive empire that spanned all of Europe and into the Middle East.

A central pillar of Roman might resided in their military, which cultivated absolute group cohesion above all else. Recruits were taken young, and joined together into groups of eight that stayed together for years. These teammates weren't just training partners; they also played and lived together. A major tenet of the Roman training regime was to instill in you not just how special you were, but also how special all of your teammates were. The idea was that by turning your organization into your family, legionnaires would fight fiercely to protect each other and not worry about failing to return home to loved ones. After all, their loved ones were on the battlefield with them.

These cohesive ties permeated not just the military, but the ruling class as well. Roman government was a family affair, with nearly all major leaders related to each other in some way. However, as the empire expanded, maintaining this cohesion couldn't be done through blood alone. New territories had to be similarly incorporated into the Roman fold, and this was done by literally developing a shared language. In their schooling the ruling elite spent nearly a decade studying the same four authors (Cicero, Sallust, Terence, and Virgil). Next they were instructed on proper language use, which meant speaking and writing exactly as the masters did centuries prior. Only the ruling class used such language, and it was immediately clear whether one was part of the "in-group" or an imposter. The cultural norms were simply too difficult to imitate.

Along with the empire's expansion came changes in the highest seat of power—the emperor. Although no emperor ruled in Rome's early history as a republic, later in its existence it became a critical role in the government. As the head of state, the emperor had to maintain close ties with regional governors because they had to understand how to execute the empire's policies while at the same time stem revolt from their domain. This meant that the emperor was often traveling from city to city on official visits. As the empire grew larger, his absence from Rome grew longer and longer.

This travel soon became impractical, and it was deemed necessary, unofficially, to have at least two emperors governing different parts of the empire. However, because the empire was so large, emperors were still spending nearly all of their time traveling. Subjects all across the empire now considered themselves full Romans, with the inherent rights that came along with it. However, these different regions still had different customs, even different languages. Cohesiveness was threatened not only in the general populace, but in the governing class as well.

The fundamentals of Rome had changed. Although other factors were also involved, the Roman Empire soon unceremoniously collapsed under its own weight.[3] Still, the principles of centralized control, cohesiveness, and formalized procedures endured in governments and organizations, remaining more or less unchanged until the 1800s and the explosion of modern industry.

Talkin' 'Bout a Revolution

The industrial revolution had a profound impact on management. Although most of us think of the industrial revolution as a period of technological innovation, changes in management over this period also still endure. In many ways, the genesis of what we recognize as a modern organization developed during this period, and the basic inventions that were developed formed the foundation for modern society. Modern paper manufacturing has its origins in the industrial revolution, as does gas lighting and the steam engine. Although these and other inventions had lasting effects, the steam engine is what would directly impact management.

Steam power immediately changed the mining industry and revolutionized transportation with the locomotive and steamboat. This transportation innovation was particularly important because it allowed people to travel extremely quickly over large distances. Rather than taking weeks to travel across Europe, the journey could be completed by train in a few days. The Atlantic could be crossed in a similarly short period of time, enhancing the flow of goods and ideas.

Companies could actually collaborate with people in different parts of the world, but this also brought about new challenges. How can you transfer effective manufacturing processes to different plants? What types of organizational structures are necessary to manage a diverse workforce spread across the world?

As goods and raw materials could be transported in large quantities relatively quickly, companies that could mass-produce goods thoroughly trounced smaller and less-nimble competitors on everything from quality to price. The factory was central to this overall strategy. Whereas, in the past, manufacturing had consisted of a few highly trained artisans laboriously constructing goods, factory production was made up of an army of low-skilled workers who each were specifically trained to complete a single task.

Division of labor was crucial for the effectiveness of a factory. By dividing production into small, independent steps, companies could turn out huge quantities of high-quality goods with these low-skilled workers. However, companies up to that point had not been set up to optimize those kinds of organizations. Well into the 1800s, most people worked in some form of master/apprentice relationship. In order to learn a trade such as carpentry, for example, you would literally live with a master for years, sometimes decades, in order to hone your skill. These businesses looked a lot more like art houses than companies.

New theories had to be developed to ensure that these factory workforces were as efficient and productive as possible. In the late 1800s, Frederick Taylor attempted to apply a rigorous analytical method to these manufacturing processes, developing a framework called scientific management—more commonly known today as Taylorism. His approach focused on measuring differences in performance between workers, observing how the most productive people did their job, and then standardizing that process and disseminating it across the organization.

Taylorism views people as cogs in a machine, with some cogs working better than others. In this model no room exists for a creative or knowledgeable worker. The goal instead is to squeeze the most amount of work out of your employees and ensure that inefficiencies are reduced as much as possible. This typically resulted in harder, longer work hours for the low-level employees and a huge amount of power in the hands of management.

Financially speaking, this approach made a lot of sense for factories of that time period. The vast majority of work *was* unskilled, and with a huge influx of immigrants into the West, creating a cohesive workforce would have been extremely difficult. When you have thousands of employees working on exactly the same process, discovering what makes people effective and transferring it across the organization is clearly important.

Chinks in Taylorism's armor became apparent almost immediately. While pushing relentlessly toward increased efficiency, companies ignored the physical and mental needs of their workers. In the United Kingdom, for example, the Factory Act of 1819 magnanimously limited child labor to 12 hours per day. No minimum age was set for child workers until 1833, when children under the age of 9 were banned from working in the textiles industry.

Unfortunately, workers had no way to effectively protest these conditions. Many early attempts at strikes were easily put down by management. With a huge potential labor pool all clamoring for jobs, any workers who went on strike were summarily fired and replaced. Because these jobs were relatively unskilled, not many concerns existed about the cost of retraining.

This attitude galvanized workers to devise a response that would give them some leverage against management. Their answer was to form trade unions. The idea was that by banding together thousands of workers from a variety of disciplines, workers could effectively blockade companies that offered poor compensation or working conditions. Although unions were illegal in the early 1800s and severely discouraged later on, they gradually became a powerful force in organizational life.

This *détente* between workers and management continued for decades, rising in importance during both world wars and creating a manufacturing dynamo in the United States. People could look forward to working their entire lives for a single company, ensured of a job no matter the economic conditions. In fact, this system by and large still exists in some countries today, particularly in large companies in Japan.

From a practical perspective, this meant that you came to know the people you worked with remarkably well. Not only did you spend decades working with the same people, but people typically spent large amounts of their personal time with their colleagues. Blue-collar workers were expected to join unions and participate in union events, whereas white-collar workers joined social clubs and fraternal organizations. Ironically, this arrangement mimicked the way that people had worked earlier in history. Like the master/apprentice relationship and hunting tribes, the vast majority of workers in the mid-twentieth century were still heavily engaged with their colleagues.

Throughout this time, however, blue-collar workers were still treated as interchangeable parts. Even people in creative industries such as advertising and research were managed in much the same way as factory workers. Managing to enhance individual creativity and increase job satisfaction was a relatively novel idea well into the 1970s.

This model started to shift, however, when companies in Japan started to outcompete their Western rivals. Toyota introduced their eponymous Toyota Production System (TPS) in the late 1940s, but it didn't rise to the attention of the international business community until the late 1970s. It was during this time that Toyota started to make major inroads into Western markets, eating market share from the likes of GM and Ford with superior quality cars and lower prices.

When managers and researchers looked for the impetus of this change, they stumbled upon the TPS. The TPS treats even front-line workers as an integral part of the development process. Workers are encouraged to develop their own methods and feed them back to the company. Toyota also urges their employees to think of themselves as part of a team, making sure that they're involved and care about the people they work with.

The Toyota Production System was subsequently adopted in many industries across the world. Although saying that the popularity of this system directly led to widespread acceptance of the importance of collaboration would be an exaggeration, it was definitely a contributor. Companies started to think about the importance of getting people talking, of having a workforce that was constantly improving. Interestingly, this way of thinking didn't lead to more talking face to face, but heavier use of a new technology called e-mail.

New Information, New Communication

E-mail was invented in 1971[4] as a way to quickly exchange information over the burgeoning Internet. At first e-mail was limited to academic circles and could only be used for text communication. It wasn't until the 1980s that images and documents could be attached to a message, and that's when e-mail really took off. Prior to e-mail, the only way to disseminate information across an entire company was to send a memo. E-mail is nearly instantaneously transmitted and enables a rapid back-and-forth between participants.

The adoption of e-mail and IT systems in general in the corporate world led to a rapid increase in productivity. Erik Brynjolfsson from MIT showed that from the late 1980s to the late 1990s, every dollar companies spent on new IT systems such as e-mail increased that company's value by $12 by changing how people could collaborate at a massive scale.

Around the same time, the use of the Web for business was exploding. In the early '80s, imagining the extent of the impact the Web would have might have been hard, but it was already having a profound effect on the way that companies worked. The Web truly democratized information gathering, giving employees sitting at their computers the ability to search through records and understand what was happening in their market in real time. This capability was one of the major catalysts for the ever-accelerating changes that have occurred in the way companies work.

The proliferation of mobile phones built on this trend, and in the early 2000s the "Crackberry" addiction had the corporate world in its grasp. Working in concert with the remote work trend, cellphone-based e-mail became a staple of business in the U.S., but it also changed the way people work. Today, we can be "always on," and never truly separated from work. Although this availability allows organizations and employees to be more flexible, it also means they start spending more time on cellphones than talking to people face-to-face.

Instant messaging (IM) also has had an impact on work styles. Whether it happens on cellphones or on computers, IM solves many of the issues associated with e-mail. It's a synchronous communication channel, meaning that you're engaged in a conversation rather than in letter passing. This feature has made it an indispensable communication medium, particularly in the technology community, where IM has been integrated into most of the software and technological development systems in use today.

IMs are also more expressive than e-mails. Where proper e-mail etiquette demands that you choose words carefully because they can be easily forwarded to thousands of other people, IMs are more ephemeral, and misspelling words and using emoticons are the norm. IMs are also much better than e-mail at exchanging nuanced information. Because any chat is a conversation, you can quickly ask for confirmation on a particular point and ensure that you're on the same page. However, IMs are not so good at connecting people who don't know each other or at coordinating more than a few people at the same time.

Until recently, air travel was the primary way to make these new contacts. Today video conferencing has been put up as a cheap alternative. Companies inherently understand that face time is important, but in a globalized world, being physically present everywhere you're needed is impossible. While in smaller organizations one-on-one video chats are fairly popular, in larger companies they're mostly used for meetings. They are definitely a step above telephone calls, because they can convey facial expressions and give you a sense of the environment. However, issues exist with communication lag and the inability to look someone in the eye when you're talking to them (you can look directly at the camera, but then you can't see the other person on the screen).

Some technological fixes are available for these problems. A great example is Cisco's telepresence solution. Its system is actually an enclosed room that consists of some chairs positioned around a half table attached to a massive screen. When the system is running, high-resolution cameras and speakers seamlessly connect you to an identical room in another location. The experience is quite remarkable, because it really does replicate the feel of a face-to-face meeting, minus the handshake. Unfortunately, this system costs hundreds of thousands of dollars and is still only good for scheduled meetings, not general socialization.

The Organization of Today

With the plethora of tools available today, people can work more effectively, communicate more quickly, and be flexible with the way they spend their time. Companies today are organized to take advantage of these tools, which enables rapid change in the products and services that they offer. In many ways, this has brought about changes in the workforce as well. You no longer can expect to be employed at a single company your entire life, because your skills in fast-growing fields such as engineering, design, and software development will most likely not be applicable in 10 years.

With this change in the employee-company relationship, people have become incredibly mobile in their careers. Switching jobs every few years is now a completely normal occurrence, and in some circles staying in one company too long is actually frowned upon. The tight cohesiveness of workforces that was the norm in previous decades is to a large extent a thing of the past.

With this increased job mobility, an increase in geographic mobility has followed. Because people are moving jobs about once every 10 years, over a typical 40-year career you'll go through at least four jobs. This makes setting down roots in a city and expecting to stay there for your entire life difficult. In fact, over their lifetimes, U.S. citizens live in an average of three different cities.[5] Compare this change to just a few decades ago, when the vast majority of people lived in the city of their birth for most of their lives.

The geographic mobility issue is compounded by what academia frequently calls the "two-body problem." Whereas in the 1950s, '60s, and '70s rates of working women were relatively low, that percentage has skyrocketed over time, representing 47% of the U.S. workforce today.[6] Now all serious relationships have a complicating factor: Both partners can find a job that requires them to move. Rather than having to concern ourselves with four job changes, now we're looking at eight.

Some people think this "two-body problem" is new. Indeed, career mobility itself is quite a new concept. However, families across history have had to contend with both a man and a woman, if not children, working to make ends meet. Prior to the twentieth century, men and women working in those low-paying factories and on farms had to work long hours so that their meager wages could provide for their family. Although a small number of wealthy individuals could support a household with only one partner working, this was the exception rather than the rule.

The period between approximately 1920 and 1975 was a singular moment in time when one family member was the primary caregiver.[7] This arrangement enabled men to socialize with one another after work, a necessary social glue that previously had been provided by shared experience at work and life together in villages in pre-industrial periods.

Now let's shift back to the present. Old social norms that value collaboration and relationships have been revived, but coordination of jobs between partners has gotten much more difficult. These conditions, in large part, provided impetus for the burgeoning remote work movement.

The growing power of information technology provides people the option of working remotely. At first making heavy use of e-mail, telephone, and quick in-and-outs on an airplane, remote work today consists more of video conferences and instant messaging exchanges. While making use of cutting-edge technology to communicate, our methods of actually managing companies still look very similar to organizations from the 1950s. We rely heavily on formal organizational methods to deal with a workforce that has drastically more mobility, technical savvy, and a pressing need for collaboration to tackle increasingly complex work.

That's where we are today. However, this historical and evolutionary perspective doesn't provide insight into how organizations are actually run. Although we all work in organizations, most of us don't know how they're put together and what makes them tick.

This chapter has looked at how the concept of an organization developed over time, starting with informal groups, which grew into city-states and governments, and then more recently into the concept of corporations. Today, all three of these organizational forms still exist as families, modern governments, and millions of companies spread across the world.

Naturally, these organizations are all structured differently. People intuitively know that a school shouldn't be organized like a government, nor should a family be organized like a company. This book focuses on companies, but even in that specific case, what "organizing" actually means can get fairly complicated.

(In)formal Processes

Broadly speaking, there are two aspects to managing an organization: formal and informal processes. Formal processes are all the things that are written down that determine how the organization works and how things get done. They are codified and ideally executed according to a written plan. There's no room in these plans for variation between people or parts of the organization unless they are explicitly specified. Although this definition might be an idealized view of how companies operate, formal processes have been a major focus of management and management scholars.

Informal processes are everything else. They're the things you learn (or don't learn) by being inside the organization. Things such as culture, tacit knowledge, and social norms fall under the purview of informal process.

Let's focus on a few of the most important processes, the ones that most people deal with every day.

Lingua Franca

Although it might seem trivial, as we shift toward a more global society, organizations have an important decision to make about what language they speak. While today English is essentially the international language, what language do people speak when an international company such as Google opens an office in a non-English-speaking country?

Adopting a lingua franca simplifies collaboration across cultural boundaries. Because everyone speaks the same language, you can naturally jump into conversations that you hear in the hallway or join another group's meeting. This ease of collaboration is extremely important as a company first moves into a new country, because a number of people from the company's headquarters are usually present to ensure that the new branch setup runs smoothly and to train new employees. However, enforcing a particular language also slows communication between team members from the same culture because fluency levels will vary.

Conversely, allowing local languages to be spoken speeds expansion in new locales after the initial setup phase because new employees can be trained in their native language. It also grows the available talent pool, because even in highly developed countries reaching a business level of fluency in a foreign language is difficult. The challenge in these organizations comes from trying to integrate workers into the fabric of the larger company. Employees from different branches have to communicate through formal channels to get things done due to language difficulties, and people speaking different languages won't be able to informally chat around the office.

The lingua franca decision is often made by a strong collaboration between human resources departments and upper management, because these choices will drive the personnel dynamics of the company.

Dollars, Sense, and Workflow

Human resources departments across the world exist for a few specific purposes: to hire, evaluate, oversee, and pay employees. Each one of these represents a formal process in an organization. While this list isn't exhaustive, these items serve as a good starting point for the purposes of this discussion.

Many people have a negative opinion of employee evaluation. The stereotypical view of evaluation involves employees nervously fidgeting as they wait for their boss to finish leisurely flipping through a performance report, at which point their boss rips into them and tells them why they shouldn't be promoted, given a bonus, and so on.

However, evaluation isn't just an opportunity for determining bonuses. It's a way to help people figure out what needs to change to perform better and to understand what they're doing well.

This point is usually overlooked. Too often, "evaluation" is used as a euphemism for "criticism." This is unfortunate, because this is only part of what evaluation should be. A better term would be "feedback." Good feedback helps people identify the things they're doing wrong while at the same time pointing out strengths. For example, if you're a good organizer but have trouble responding to requests in a timely fashion, then moving forward you have a very clear action plan. You should take a more active role in management and group leadership, because you'll make the whole team more effective, but you should also make extensive use of your calendar to ensure you're meeting your communication requirements.

Continuing on this point, evaluation is also used to figure out how roles should change over time. Maybe your skill set is better suited for another division, or you've been identified as high potential and will start being groomed for an upper management role. These assignments can't be made on a whim. A regular, well-thought-out process should be in place for determining how to move people along in their career.

In most organizations the results of evaluation also directly impact how people get paid. Though it seems obvious that companies need to monetarily reward their employees, many careers focus relatively little on material rewards and instead make the organizational mission a reward in itself. This is particularly true in non-profit organizations. People in careers supporting worthy causes such as suicide prevention and caring for the homeless don't bring home big paychecks, but because they are so passionate about the mission of the company, they're willing to tough it out.

Determining incentives, however, is not straightforward. You can pay employees with commissions, pay them hourly, or hire them full time and pay bonuses. The type of compensation you choose is inextricably tied to the type of work people do and the type of work you want them to do.

We think of hiring people full time for a fixed salary as the default employment arrangement for white-collar careers. Fixed salaries are designed to make people more committed to an organization and ensure that changing work demands don't become an issue. A company that hires a person full time is committing to his or her long-term development and signaling that this is someone they would like to be deeply involved in the organization. Although full-time employees aren't eligible for overtime, they're also not docked pay when things are slow. This represents a significant investment by the company, because if they consistently overestimate how much work needs to be done, the result is a lot of extra money spent on salaries.

Hourly employees, on the other hand, are much better for ramping up and down with demand. This pattern is common in retail during holiday seasons or at restaurants during high load times such as lunch and dinner hours. The downside of hourly wages is that employees aren't as ingrained in the organization because companies are wary of providing extra training to workers who won't necessarily be around long term. This arrangement also reduces the social integration of workers because they have to be focused on immediate output or risk losing their jobs. Schmoozing with coworkers by the coffee machine, unfortunately, nearly becomes a firable offense.

Bonuses and commissions are mostly used as a supplement to full-time and hourly arrangements, although in certain industries such as consulting and upper management, commissions and bonuses can make up the lion's share of take-home pay. Bonuses fall into a few classes based on how they are awarded: individual performance, group performance, and company performance.

Many of us are familiar with the concept of individual bonuses. These bonuses are designed to incentivize people to complete their own work to the best of their ability and to go above and beyond the call of duty. Individual bonuses are typically based on an evaluation of your performance, either qualitatively by your superiors or through hard productivity numbers. A challenge with individual bonuses is that they tend to make people inwardly focused and disinterested in helping their colleagues, because the time they spend on those interactions doesn't show up in their paychecks.

Commissions are a special case of individual bonuses. A commission gives you a percentage or flat dollar amount for every sale an employee makes. This applies in retail stores where employees get commissions for selling merchandise, all the way up to partners of large consulting firms, who typically get commissions by closing big customer contracts.

Group bonuses are designed to get teams to collaborate and hit overall performance targets. This is often useful when rewarding an individual on his or her contribution is impossible because it's part of a larger product or service. By rewarding people at the group level, companies encourage people to work together to solve problems rather than look at just their own work. These bonuses are often used in software development to incentivize teams to hit their delivery date. Although an employee's code might be only a small fraction of the overall software, he'll try harder to jump in and help other parts of the team that are falling behind to get the bonus.

The downside to these bonuses is that they can lead to free-riding because lower-performing employees get paid the same as the high performers. Lower performers can be content to coast by, knowing that someone else will pick up the slack and they'll still get their bonus. If this pattern of behavior becomes prevalent, it will severely demotivate the highest performers and further degrade group performance.

Company performance can also be used to determine bonuses. This practice is typically called profit sharing, and is designed to encourage collaboration not just across a specific team, but across the entire organization. Similar to group bonuses, the main idea behind profit sharing is that because your bonus depends on other parts of the company, you'll try to branch out and pitch in across a wide variety of areas to ensure that the company succeeds. The problems with these bonuses mirror those of group bonuses, because there's no good way to reward individuals based on their individual effort.

Even the type of pay people take home is a compensation lever. Rather than pay cash, companies could pay employees in stock. Startup companies usually take this route because they lack the cash to pay an employee's full salary, but it's also common practice for paying CEOs of large companies. By receiving stock rather than cash, employees are invested in the long-term future of the company, because if the company does well down the road, the stock will be worth more. This is an important point for CEOs because it ensures that they don't sell off important parts of the company to make a quick buck while eviscerating the company in the long term. The downside is that employees usually can't sell this stock for a long period of time, so for lower-level employees being paid in company stock doesn't necessarily provide more incentive than a cash bonus or salary.

This discussion hasn't even gotten into complicated pay schemes. Suffice it to say that companies can mix these different compensation schemes and make bonuses and salary hikes dependent on certain benchmarks or performance goals, but at the end of the day, it has to be simple. The more complicated a scheme, the less likely an employee is to understand it, so it will be less likely to have the desired effect on their behavior. The takeaway is that evaluation and incentive mechanisms are organizational levers that can change the way people work.

Having a process for making these decisions so that you know you're rewarding the right behavior is important. That usually means that there should be a formal process around compensation decisions. Creating a workflow process around this and other organizational issues is a necessity if you're going to run an effective company.

Every meeting that pops up on your calendar is part of a formal workflow process. Workflow means going through all the items on a checklist and making sure that you hit them in order. Although in most cases workflow doesn't actually take the form of a checklist, most processes could be boiled down into this general framework.

Take budget planning as an example. The relevant people first need a brainstorming session to hash out the division's needs for the year. Team members are each assigned to manage the budget for different areas, so before the next meeting they'll have to accurately assess the needs of individual areas under their purview. After a few iterations, the division will be ready to present its budget proposal to the higher-ups, which will have a similar process of their own.

Especially in modern organizations, managing workflow has become critical. With people working on ever more complex projects, it's necessary to set regular meetings and milestones and use reporting tools to make sure that everyone is coordinated. To ensure this coordination happens in a timely manner, an organization needs a defined set of people who can make these decisions. As in the budgeting example, defined contact points must exist so that things can keep moving forward. This is the purpose of the org chart, the company hierarchy.

When you think about the formal part of a company, the org chart is probably the first thing that comes to mind. Many factors go into figuring out the best way to structure these reporting relationships. Do you need to coordinate with different groups? How many subordinates can you reasonably oversee? This is one of the most important parts of the formal processes of organizations, and as you might suspect, there's not one "right way" to do it.

Choosing a Company Structure

Making sure that the right groups are coordinating is essential for having a successful organization. These reporting relationships are a big part of that coordination. One of the reasons for the wild success of organizations in the early twentieth century was the hierarchies and systems of control they put in place. Knowing that a particular individual or group of individuals is ultimately going to have the final say is important because it helps you figure out who you need to talk to, who you're accountable to, and who to go to when you need access to resources.

There are roughly four ways to structure these reporting relationships. Companies can mix and match them for different parts of the organization, but doing so is not the norm because it makes understanding the structure and managing the overall organization considerably more difficult. The basic idea is to pick the organizational structure that best supports the overall organizational strategy.

Functional Management

The functional management structural style organizes people around the type of work they do. Consider a global restaurant chain. Under a functional management regime, it would have a division for food procurement and distribution, a restaurant division that runs the individual establishments, a research and development division for coming up with new menu offerings, and a marketing division.

Functional management allows people to focus on their specific part of the business and tends to create economies of scale in terms of implementation and process optimization. In a functional organization, for example, all distribution activities are centralized, meaning that managers can figure out the best way to optimize distribution across different locations. One potential issue with functional management is that it tends to create solutions that aren't tailored for specific markets. The only way different locations get different offerings is for that information to percolate up the hierarchy and then filter back down to R&D. Next these new innovations would have to go back up the chain from R&D and down to the restaurants for them to actually be implemented on the ground.

Divisional Management

Divisional management takes a different tack by organizing reporting relationships into self-contained units that include everything necessary to do a job. This structure is often used in industries that have to customize their products for different locations, like the restaurant and retail industries. A restaurant chain would look very different under a divisional structure. In this case, it would have a U.S. division, a European division, a Japanese division, and a South American division. Each division would have its own R&D, its own distribution channels, and its own marketing teams.

Divisional organizations tend to be much more flexible than their functional counterparts. Because they are specifically attuned to the needs and opportunities in their individual segments, different divisions can offer different products and services. Unfortunately, this often means a large duplication of effort across divisions because the company now has four R&D divisions, four distribution channels, and four marketing teams. Not only does this mean more staff, but also that coordinating campaigns and product development across divisions becomes extremely difficult.

Matrixed Management

The matrixed organizational form tries to combine the best of both the functional and divisional structures. This structure is organized across multiple dimensions to try to ensure coordination across different organizational silos but still maintain flexibility. The idea is that instead of reporting to just one manager, you now report to both a functional and a divisional manager. In the restaurant example, this could mean that an employee might have a boss from Japan and a boss from marketing.

A major benefit of matrixed organizations is that they allow for cost savings by centralizing different functions but can quickly innovate in different areas by aggregating information from across the company. The cost of this system is higher in two areas: complexity and time. Matrixed organizations are much more complex than their functional or divisional counterparts. Some organizations even matrix across more than two dimensions; for example, product, geography, and function. This complexity makes changing the organizational structure after it's set up difficult.

As you can imagine, in a matrixed organization a lot of time must be devoted to communicating with bosses. This is not necessarily a bad thing, because coordination across organizational silos is usually extremely important. What this creates, however, is a lot of formal processing that has to occur before an initiative can start. Instead of a single boss giving the okay, now people from very different areas must be on the same page and approve the initiative.

Teams

Teams are often put up as a lightweight alternative to matrixing. Although teams have existed for a long time, only recently have they become a critical part of organizational structure. Traditionally sitting outside of the org chart, they are nonetheless a critical organizing factor and exhibit similar properties to matrixed organizations. Teams are typically tasked with accomplishing a specific set of objectives and often have an internal organizational structure along functional lines, although the scale is obviously smaller. In some organizations teams work on a specific project, such as a new aircraft or piece of software, and can persist for years.

The teams referred to in this discussion are small teams, because if a team gets beyond roughly 20 people, it becomes in essence a temporary division. Teams can be effective because they enable people from different backgrounds to collaborate and understand the strengths and challenges of different parts of the organization. When teams break out from traditional constraints, their output can be much more innovative than that generated within a specific division. This uniqueness, however, can also be a source of trouble. Getting team members on the same page might take a long time, if they ever do, and many teams find themselves working through individual conflicts rather than working together toward their real goal.

So, We're Done Learning About Organizations, Right?

What's interesting about the org chart is that most companies operate as if all communication occurs across its lines. From this perspective, if you don't directly connect with someone, you don't need to talk with him or her.

This is one area where traditional management theory breaks down. Many of us have worked, and we know that talking to other people on your team is also important. They don't report to you, you don't report to them, but you need to touch base and coordinate to be effective.

This coordination is an informal process. Your informal communication, be it chatting at the coffee machine or eating lunch together, are all important informal processes.

Informally Important

Informal processes are all about the culture of the organization. These aren't things that you'll learn about in a training manual. In fact, many of the things you'll read about informal processes in a manual might be completely wrong.

A big part of informal processes are social norms, which guide your behavior not just at work but throughout your life. For example, if your family spends lots of time outside playing basketball, then your family has a social norm around sports. Social norms at school could involve reading during free periods or making a habit of interrupting class when the teacher is talking. Simply put, social norms are the things you do because everyone is doing them.

These norms are extremely important, because they keep behavior predictable and, ideally, optimized to some desirable end state. You know when you come into work that people won't be sitting naked on their desks watching soap operas because there are norms against that. Similarly, you also know that your colleagues are going to get that urgent report done because the norm is to complete the work even if people have to do it from home.

These social conventions determine important things about the organization, like where people eat lunch, how employees talk to each other, and what "business casual" really means. What's interesting about these norms is that they often emerge spontaneously. Although managers might try to shape them, doing it is notoriously difficult because quantifying these things is so hard.

For example, consider where people eat lunch. A lot of factors contribute to your decision about where to eat. If everyone eats at their desk, then chances are you'll eat at your desk. If everyone goes out to eat, then you probably will as well. You might also go out to lunch because your friends do, or because food in the cafeteria is so good (or cheap—cheap food being a great motivator).

Ironically, the formality of a workplace is an important aspect of organizational culture. This appears in not only the way people talk but also in the way they dress. These norms are often partially formally specified, in terms of dress codes and gossip policies, but the way they actually manifest themselves is by and large an informal process.

Talking about personal lives at work can be a major point of contention within a company. Having a strong norm against discussing personal situations can ensure that messy personal issues don't take over the office and helps people focus on their work. On the other hand, this creates barriers in the company that can negatively impact mental health and performance. For example, if someone were having marital problems, it would invariably affect them at work. Without being able to talk about this with colleagues, the person's stress level could increase and have negative effects on the whole team.

The formality of dress can have a similar effect. Although suits and "professional" dress can promote a respectable atmosphere for clients, they also promote conformity. Researchers have found, for example, that pedestrians are more likely to violate traffic laws if they see a person wearing a suit doing it versus someone in jeans and a t-shirt.

The Social Network

The discussion so far has tiptoed around what actually constitutes the social fabric of an organization. This chapter has covered in vague terms what groups and relationships are, but really hasn't pinned this down into something measurable. Social scientists for centuries had the same problem, and it wasn't until the 1930s that a solution was posed in the form of an oft-abused term: social networks.

The social network construct is a way for scientists to get a quantitative understanding of the relationships between groups. An example can help explain exactly what a social network is and why it is such an important tool.

Imagine five people, represented in Figure 2.1 with dots.

Figure 2.1 Five people

Now, suppose you want to show that one person is friends with another person. A simple way to do this is to draw a line from one dot to another as shown in Figure 2.2.

Figure 2.2 Two friends

If you wanted to show not just one relationship, but lots of relationships, you would get a diagram that looks something like Figure 2.3.

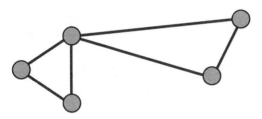

Figure 2.3 Multiple relationships

Now suppose you didn't want to look at friendships, but who talks to each other. In that case, the diagrams might differ from week to week. One week you could get a pattern like you see in Figure 2.3, but the next week you could get something like that shown in Figure 2.4.

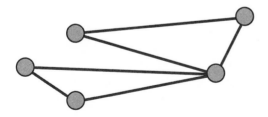

Figure 2.4 People communicating

Taking this example further, what if you wanted to show not just who talks to whom, but also how much they talk to each other? You could do this by making the lines thinner or thicker depending on who was talking, as shown in Figure 2.5 (two of the nodes are shaded to use in a later discussion).

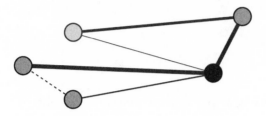

Figure 2.5 Showing communication amount

A few questions can be answered when looking at this diagram. The first is simple: How many people does each person talk to? You can answer this by counting the number of lines touching each dot. In a social network, this is called the *degree*. The light gray dot has a degree of two, whereas the black dot has a degree of four.

Degree, however, is a simple measure for which you don't really need a social network. For more complicated measures, you need some way to mathematically represent a network. Luckily, these kinds of diagrams have been used in a field of mathematics called graph theory. In graph theory, dots and lines are represented in a matrix, which is essentially a table of numbers. To understand what this looks like, let's consider a very simple social network, shown in Figure 2.6.

Figure 2.6 Another simple network

In this graph the dot (or *node* in the mathematical jargon) A is connected to nodes B and C. Mathematically, this is represented by the following matrix:

	A	B	C
A	–	1	1
B	1	–	0
C	1	0	–

In this example, the matrix is just the grid of nine entries in this table. Entry BA is 1, because you know that nodes B and A talk to each other. BC and CB, however, are set to 0 because B and C don't talk to each other. In this matrix, you don't pay attention to the entries AA, BB, and CC because that would represent someone talking to themselves (which, while humorous, isn't something discussed here).

Importantly, these entries don't have to be just one and zero. Suppose you want to show how much people communicated with each other? You could then have a matrix where the entries represent how many minutes each person talked to each other. For example, Figure 2.7 would be represented by the following matrix:

	A	B	C
A	–	20	3
B	20	–	0
C	3	0	–

Figure 2.7 A simple network with communication amounts

In this matrix you can see that A and B talk for 20 minutes, while A and C talk only for 3 minutes. This representation makes an easy task of encoding not just who talks to whom, but also how much. Time, however, isn't easily captured here. To look at a network over time, you would actually have to look at many matrices, one for each time period.

With the matrix concept under your belt, let's see what you can do with this data. You now know about degree, and a computer can easily calculate degree from a matrix. It just counts how many non-zero entries are in that node's row.

However, a matrix allows you to do so much more. One major concept used in this book is *cohesion*. Cohesion is a way to measure how tightly knit someone's network is. Conceptually, it measures how much the people you talk to talk to each other, placing more emphasis on the people you speak the most with. Take, for example, Figure 2.8.

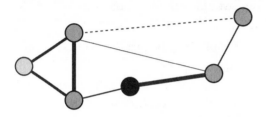

Figure 2.8 Yet another social network

Compare the networks of the gray and black nodes. The light gray node talks to two other people, who spend the vast majority of their time talking to each other or the gray node. The black node, on the other hand, talks to two people who don't talk at all to each other. The cohesion of the light gray node would be very high, while that of the black node would be 0.

The last big concept used in this book is the idea of *centrality*, specifically *betweenness centrality*. Take a look back at Figure 2.5.

You immediately notice that there are two groups of people, and the black node is the only one who connects the two groups. This makes that person very important, because they're the only way for information to get from one group to the other. Later chapters will discuss the implications, but for now it's not hard to understand that people in these high centrality positions are generally more powerful, influential, and learn about things faster than other people.

Mathematically, you measure betweenness centrality by trying to make "paths" through the network. Imagine that the nodes represent cities and the lines represent roads between the cities. You can only drive on the roads that are already there, and for the purposes of this discussion consider the roads to all be equal in length. To get from one place to another, you just need to find the path that takes you on the smallest number of roads.

Centrality measures what percentage of time each node is on that shortest path for every pair of nodes in the network. In the example, every shortest path from a node in one group to a node in a different group would have to go through the black node, and so its centrality would be by far the highest.

Applying this concept to organizations, you can make a social network diagram with all the people who work in a company. As you might imagine, the pattern of these connections has profound implications for how information flows and how work gets done. Studies throughout this book will use the Sociometric Badges, e-mail data, and other information to measure these social networks and investigate their relationship with outcomes that people care about, such as productivity and job satisfaction. After all, despite the discussion of these organizing mechanisms and informal processes, that's what you want to improve.

Organizing the Path Ahead

This chapter covered the basics of formal and informal processes, but by no means was the discussion exhaustive. To adequately go into all that detail would take another book.

This chapter does, however, lay the framework for what's to come. Chapter 1 covered how data can correct some of the problems inherent in how we understand organizations today. Now that you have a sense of what fundamentally comprises a company, you can venture into the world of organizations armed with a better understanding of that nebulous concept and, more importantly, data.

3

The Water Cooler Effect
Why a Friendly Chat Is the Most
Important Part of the Work Day

After you get sensing data, what should you analyze first? You could go after org charts, meetings, or compensation systems, but investigating something basic would be better, something fundamental to what it means to be human—such as water. For example, look at the ubiquitous source of water in offices across the world: the water cooler.

Buying a water cooler is the single most important investment a company can make. Well, maybe that's overstating things a bit, but not by much (and no, this is not a commercial plug that Poland Springs®, makers of the finest water coolers available, paid for me to put in this book).

The reason that water coolers are so important isn't just that they slake our thirst for cool, refreshing H_2O, but rather that they create a nexus of social activity in the workplace. Water coolers are where you bump into people in the office that you haven't seen in a while, and they're where you gossip about coworkers or talk about last night's game. They serve a crucial social function that desks and meeting rooms can't provide.

Although this discussion focuses on water coolers, really any watering hole in the office has similar effects. Coffee machines, kitchens, cafes, and recreational areas provide a similar environment that can greatly enhance social connectivity in the workplace.

Sadly, in the vast majority of companies the water cooler is an afterthought, relegated to some corner where there happens to be a spare power outlet. The location of the water cooler isn't a topic of discussion at the higher levels of management, and usually is decided based on where there's enough space to put it, rather than using it to facilitate interaction.

This practice indicates a broader problem in workplaces. Companies rarely think about the things that aren't formal aspects of work, but spend years crafting org charts, setting up IT systems, and planning organizational strategy. They should be spending time doing those things. They're critical components for every major company in the world. The point is that communication and collaboration also need some attention.

Talk Your Ear Off

Organizations are a way to get people to collaborate with each other. Companies can make software, airplanes, and cutlery because they're able to get a group of people to work together on the millions of things that make up these products. People have just formalized collaboration into org charts, processes, and memos.

We collaborate by passing information to one another. We can communicate using e-mail, phone calls, or talking to each other face-to-face, but no one in the history of work has ever created an organization where people can collaboratively make a product with no communication. In some sense, you could argue that if people are "collaborating" on a product and not talking to each other, then they are actually making separate products that work in tandem. This is equivalent to a person who makes light bulbs and a person who makes a lamp. You can't use one without the other, but those people don't need to talk to each other to each make a fully functional product.

That's not to say that you need to talk with everyone at your company—far from it. If you work in a company with hundreds of thousands of employees, there's no way you can meaningfully communicate with everybody. You could send an e-mail to everyone, but you'll end up consuming hundreds of thousands of seconds for them to read that one e-mail. If everyone did that, no one would do anything but read mass e-mails all day. You could even try to communicate over the phone or face to face with as many people as possible, but at most you could have a meaningful conversation with about 100 people a day, which means that in five years at an average Fortune 500 company, you could have one five-minute conversation with every single employee.

Clearly, those two extremes don't make sense. So is it just the amount of communication that matters? That's also not the case.

Let's say you want to spend one hour of your day interacting with people. Reasonably, you should be able to use that time to talk with around 10 people. Which 10 people should you talk to? If only the amount of communication mattered, then you could pick 10 people at random from the company and speak with them every day. Obviously, in very large companies, that's pretty much a complete waste of time.

There's no way to start a conversation beyond idle chit-chat for people who don't share a common background. That's not to say chit-chat is always bad, but one hour of idle chatter every day probably doesn't make you any new friends or useful connections. You need to spend time nurturing relationships, finding a group, and communicating with your team so you have people with whom you can discuss deeper issues.

Leading thinkers and researchers are somewhat split on what this group should look like. You could have a core group of people who are all tightly connected with each other, or you could cast your net widely and talk with people who run in very different circles. Welcome to the cohesion versus diversity debate.

Cohesion versus Diversity

In this book, *cohesion* refers to the way that the people you talk to, your network, are connected with each other. A cohesive network is one where the people you talk to talk a lot to each other. If you envision a network as a web, with dots representing people and lines representing communication, then a cohesive network is one that looks like a thick tangle of string.

Most of the time when I mention diversity, I'm not talking about it in the demographic sense. For the purposes of this book, *diversity* refers to your social connections; that is, do you only talk to people who talk to each other, or do you talk to people who are in very different places in the network? A diverse network looks like a star, with many different lines emanating from you at the center, while a cohesive network looks more like a web. Figures 3.1 and 3.2 provide visual representations of what these different networks could look like.

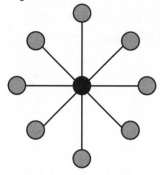

Figure 3.1 A diverse network

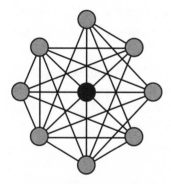

Figure 3.2 A cohesive network

The benefits of a cohesive network are best understood by looking at basketball, which is very much a team sport. Even if teams are able to cobble together players who look good on paper, there's no guarantee that talent will translate into actual wins on the court.

Can't Take the Heat

The mismatch between individual talent and team success is particularly evident in the infamous case of the 2010–2011 Miami Heat team. After the 2009–2010 basketball season, a number of high-profile basketball players had forgone contract extensions to test the open market. Among the most valuable of those free agents were three players: LeBron James, Chris Bosh, and Dwayne Wade.

Depending on whom you ask, LeBron James is one of the five best basketball players to ever play the game. His immense size, speed, and accuracy make him one of the most dangerous players on the court. He's just as comfortable mixing it up with seven-footers around the hoop as he is pulling up and hitting a three-pointer from deep outside. Almost single-handedly he made the Cleveland Cavaliers, a perennial loser in the NBA, into a basketball juggernaut. However, he was never able to close the deal in Cleveland and win a title, in large part because the roster never had any long-term star players besides LeBron.

Chris Bosh was one of the most coveted big men of the offseason. Bosh does not have the same all-time great status as LeBron, but he is a huge scoring and defensive threat, putting up impressive numbers in his seven NBA seasons and making the All-Star team five times. Like LeBron, he had languished on the Toronto Raptors, barely reaching the playoffs and never making a serious run at an NBA title.

At the same time that Bosh and James were entering the market, the Miami Heat were fighting to keep Dwayne Wade on their team. Wade is considered to be one of the best basketball players of all time, slightly behind LeBron in the overall mix, with a playing style that combines blinding speed and deadly accuracy. He had already won an NBA title by teaming up with Shaquille O'Neal in 2006, but had struggled to maintain playoff relevance after Shaq's performance started to decline.

Miami wasn't content to just hang onto Wade, however. They wanted to create a basketball powerhouse, a dynasty that would deliver a run of championships to South Beach. During the offseason, the stars had aligned where they were able to pull off the deal of the century by signing LeBron, Bosh, and Wade to long-term contracts.

The NBA makes pulling off these massive deals routinely difficult due to its salary cap structure. Each team has only a certain amount that it can spend on player salaries, with few exceptions. This required the Miami Heat to shed nearly every player they had who were not named Wade and who had a significant salary attached. To understand the depth of these cuts, of the four players who started more than half of the Heat's games in 2009–2010, only Wade remained at the start of the next season. Including substitutes, these roster changes removed players responsible for 47% of the minutes played in 2009–2010.

So despite the fact that this was a massive acquisition of top-shelf talent, at the start of the season more than half of the Heat's players were new to the team. This was a group that was not cohesive, one that would have to learn quickly in order to succeed.

The Big 3, as they came to be known, of LeBron, Wade, and Bosh, started the season with great fanfare. LeBron announced his signing in grandiose fashion in a primetime show on ESPN titled *The Decision*, proclaiming that he was "taking his talents to South Beach." The ensuing media firestorm had LeBron defending his ego-fueled television appearance and Cleveland Cavaliers fans burning his jersey in the street. At the event where they were officially introduced to Miami fans, the Big 3 promised, "not one, not two, not three, not four, not five, not six, not seven" NBA titles, but eight.

Their first campaign for the NBA title got off to an inauspicious start. After their first 17 games, the Heat could only muster an unimpressive record of 9 wins and 8 losses. This had many calling for Coach Erik Spoelstra's head. After all, how could a team with so much talent lose to a string of mediocre teams?

Those in basketball circles, however, were not fazed. ESPN analyst Hubie Brown stated: "Any coach realizes that when you bring six or seven new people to a team that is expected to play at a high level of execution, it takes time."[1] The team was just not playing in sync; but this is something that develops over time. Players need to spend time in practice working with each other to be able to anticipate how they will respond in different situations. They need to understand the small signals that people pass between each other to convey their intentions without others knowing. All of these small things add up to big results on the floor.

Not surprisingly, things finally did start to gel together for the Heat. After their 9-8 start, they rattled off 12 straight wins, and they rode this success through the playoffs into the NBA finals, where they met the much older and heavy underdog Dallas Mavericks.

The Mavericks were the anti-Heat. Where the Heat were young and a team cobbled together less than a year earlier, the Mavericks were a veteran team, led by perennial all-star Dirk Nowitzki. In stark contrast to the Heat, the Mavericks team remained mostly unchanged from the previous year, bringing back 10 players who were responsible for 80% of the team's minutes in the 2009–2010 season.

When you looked at the individual stats, however, the Mavericks shouldn't have stood a chance. On a per-game basis, the Big 3 of James, Wade, and Bosh outscored the top three players on the Mavericks by a significant margin, and as a team the Heat scored more points and gave up fewer points than the Mavericks. Strange, then, that many pundits and media outlets, from *Bleacher Report* to retired NBA legend Charles Barkley, picked the Dallas Mavericks to win. Amazingly enough, in the end it was those old Dallas Mavericks who triumphed.

This is a classic case of individual talent versus team cohesion. Miami was still improving, still getting to know each other on the floor. Dallas made up for its lack of heavy star power with a team-oriented approach. The general consensus was that Miami needed to play together more, to develop team chemistry.

The consensus was right. Miami won its championship the next year. Incidentally, that season the players who returned from the 2010–2011 squad were responsible for 81% of the team's minutes the previous year, slightly more than the former champion, the Dallas Mavericks.

Cohesion

Cohesion doesn't just work for NBA superstars and pro sports teams. These same principles impact teams in our everyday lives. Normally, the results are just much harder to see and the teams are lower profile.

A major benefit of cohesive networks is that they create high levels of trust within the group. This trust comes directly from the structure of interactions in these networks.

Let's consider a simple cohesive network, with four people who spend the vast majority of their time talking to each other. Suppose that one of those people wants to mislead someone in the group, maybe telling that person that she wasn't invited to an important meeting when in fact she was. In a non-cohesive network, or a dispersed network, it's entirely possible that no one would discover the deception.

This occurs because when you want to expose a lie, you need proof. Most of the time people are not looking for proof because the assumption is that everyone more or less tells the truth. Unless you are mistakenly forwarded an e-mail or bump into the deceiver at exactly the wrong time, you'll be entirely in the dark.

In a cohesive network, on the other hand, you receive a constant stream of information about your close contacts. People in your network are telling you about their work, what they did with other people, and so on. Because people in a cohesive network spend the majority of their time with each other, most of this information will be about your other close contacts. Similarly, you're constantly giving out information about yourself and what other people in your network are doing. If you're trying to lie, this means you have to constantly maintain the lie if you're asked about it. It also means that your lie will be thoroughly spread throughout your tight-knit network. If any one of those people discovers your deception, then everyone will know.

Very quickly you would be punished by the group, either through a stern verbal rebuke or by being ostracized. This makes the potential downside of lying very high, and especially for major issues, successfully deceiving the entire group would be extremely difficult.

Not surprisingly, when you're able to be open and trusting with a group of people, there are powerful psychological benefits. Stress in particular tends to be much lower for people who have cohesive networks. Job satisfaction also tends to be much higher for people in these groups.

The supportive effect of cohesive networks is analogous to its impact on trust. Instead of a lie, think about what happens when you tell someone in your group that you're having a bad day. One of them could even notice that you're feeling down. That information will quickly spread to everyone with whom you spend time. Pretty soon you'll have people consoling you, offering to take you out to dinner, or even just giving you a break on some of your work so you can take it easy.

You might be surprised that these interactions don't have to focus on work. In regards to trust and stress, in fact, it's probably better if people in these networks talk about their private lives in addition to their work life. This adds depth to the relationship, further enhancing trust and decreasing stress.

Some workplaces have taboos against talking about private lives, in a bid to keep things professional, but this makes a false distinction between work and home life. Having problems at home can affect you at work, and vice versa. When people go home, they think that discussing work matters is perfectly normal, but for a variety of reasons the opposite is often not true. However, not sharing information makes it difficult for people to support and work with each other effectively. Without having access to all the information, people at work might assume that you're lazy even though you're exhausted because your husband is in the hospital and you've been taking care of the kids yourself.

Sharing good news through these cohesive networks is also easy. If your work involves passing things off to people with whom you rarely speak, you probably won't see the fruits of your labor. This is particularly true in industries that don't make physical things that you can point to. If you're a programmer, for example, you might be writing one function of one program that is part of a larger system that makes up a piece of software.

By simply following the specs, you can make a passable piece of code, and if you really put your nose to the grindstone, you can produce some elegant code. After that code is integrated into the larger project, though, you probably won't have anyone thanking you for the extra work that you did. No one knows who was responsible for that particularly effective code. However, if you are in a cohesive group that is working together on this part of the project, you'll be personally thanked by grateful programmers who can appreciate how much work you put in.

This appreciation is another reason why job satisfaction tends to be higher for people in cohesive networks. After all, being happy at your job is much easier if you're working with people who help support you and also care about the work that you do.

Digging into this further, cohesive groups don't just have psychological and trust benefits; there is also a significant impact on communication effectiveness. As people in a cohesive network spend more and more time with each other, they also start to share communication shortcuts. In effect, they're developing their own language. This is not a language in a formal sense, but one in which people share common assumptions and are familiar with the same concepts.

Developing a common language is something that people do with every group with which we communicate. In your family, when you refer to "Uncle Bob," everyone knows whom you're talking about. Someone who walks off the street into your house wouldn't be able to engage in a discussion about Uncle Bob. She would lack that basic understanding.

This happens at a more complex level at work, and is particularly evident when you first join a company.

An internship I had at IBM is a good example of this phenomenon. When I first started, I had some sense of the work that was going on at the company, but I didn't know about all of their activities. Needless to say, I was confused when someone came up to me and said the following:

"Are you on beehive? We could also use same time if you don't want other people to know."

If you're an IBMer, you know what I'm talking about. *Beehive* is an internal social network at IBM, like an internal Facebook. *Same-Time* is the instant messaging program that IBM developed and uses internally. You can imagine my befuddlement when I was first confronted by this statement, but after a few weeks I was able to get some of the company lingo down. The point is that employees don't just magically know this common language when entering a company. There's a process of assimilating that information.

Company lingo is only one part of this common language. People also frequently refer to past events and organizational initiatives that you might not be familiar with. These events are typically unstated, so you find out about them almost by chance, or when one of your coworkers takes the time to explain each of these events to you.

However, these events are so culturally embedded, so inherent to the organization, that realizing that outsiders don't understand them is often difficult for employees.

In your everyday life, this can occur when you mix different groups of friends at a party. As the comedian Jim Gaffigan eloquently put it: "Don't be alarmed when you hear me speaking in a British accent." In his case, he was implying that one group of his friends knew him as British, whereas another group thought he was American. Although this is an extreme example, different groups of friends have different common events to draw on, and this can often be the cause of awkwardness when you have to constantly explain references that your friends make.

These references also take the form of common assumptions that people continually make. You might not hesitate to e-mail out a report to your whole group before your boss has a chance to take a look, but in some companies that would be frowned upon or even cause for dismissal. When talking about our work, we also make assumptions about our audience's perspective.

For example, when I was a graduate student at MIT, the idea that sensors and computers will be integrated into everyday objects such as wallets and light bulbs was very natural. We talked about these things every day, and people had long built prototypes that showed these applications were not only feasible but also very compelling. I always found it strange when a company would visit the lab and we would have to spend an hour explaining why/how you could do this. To us at MIT, it was self-evident, but to the outside world, the assumptions that we had made weren't clear at all.

A common language helps you predict how others are going to respond to you. Back during my time at MIT, a "deadline" was a fairly nebulous term that meant "have this completed in the few weeks around this date." If I took this same attitude when I worked at Hitachi, however, I would have quickly been shown the door.

If you're at a large company, having a common language is critical. Even at an institution such as MIT, I was able to walk into a meeting with people from a different department and almost immediately be on the same page. Getting this language proficiency can take weeks, even months when entering a new company. In fact, in the business world the general rule is that when you hire a new employee, you have to expect him or her to be unproductive for three months. It's not that these new employees don't come in with the necessary skills; it's that they lack the language to communicate with others.

This same problem can pop up on a project where you're collaborating with people from different parts of the organization. For a project to run smoothly, you have to get up and running quickly. If you have to spend the first three months of a six-month project working through communication issues, you're going to be in trouble.

One of the problems with the shared context people develop is that the underlying assumptions might be wrong. Research in Motion's (RIM—the company that makes the BlackBerry smartphone) declining fortunes are a vivid example of this. Even with the wild success of the first iPhone in 2007, RIM clung to the flawed assumptions that everyone wants physical keyboards, that cellphone apps were a "fad." These assumptions had been built over years of proven success. Everyone at RIM knew that the form factor of their phones was second to none. Everyone at RIM knew that you had to build better and faster hardware, but you could throw in the software and app ecosystem as an afterthought. Everyone at RIM was wrong.

These assumptions caused RIM's smartphone market share to plummet from a dominant 43% to an abysmal 12%. Why wasn't RIM able to quickly pivot and churn out an iPhone killer within a few months? After all, RIM had been making cutting-edge phones for years. Its technological innovations in software and hardware were unparalleled in the industry. The underlying issue was that RIM never questioned these basic assumptions, never allowed their context to evolve. With no data on which to base our assertions, people and companies are much more likely to go with their instinct, with what feels natural. At best, this leads to mixed results.

Enter the flip side of cohesive networks. They're also bad at a lot of things, especially when taken to extremes. As shown in the BlackBerry example, when you're in a closed-off network, discovering new information is incredibly difficult. Cohesive groups are also poor at influencing others. Because they're very inwardly focused, reaching out to different stakeholders to affect substantial change is difficult.

Diverse networks, on the other hand, are good at precisely the things that cohesive networks are not. They're structured to help us break out of old habits and change our perspective.

Diversity

We're often exhorted to break out of our comfort zone, to have new experiences. I've always thought that was incredibly unspecific. For me, breaking out of my comfort zone could mean spending eight hours at my desk staring at a monitor or drinking coffee (not my cup of tea).

Breaking out is really about doing new things and meeting new people, and the benefits of that approach have been well documented. So, if breaking out is mostly positive and cohesion is mostly positive, which is the right approach? The simple answer, although many researchers would have you believe differently, is that it isn't all or nothing. You can have a cohesive group that you spend most of your time with *and* have an extended network that you'll tap into occasionally to get new information.

Cohesiveness versus diversity is one of the most hotly debated subjects in social science. Without going into the nitty-gritty details, this debate kicked off in earnest in the 1970s with Mark Granovetter's seminal work, *The Strength of Weak Ties*. This paper showed that when you were looking for a job, the weak ties, or the people that you don't talk to very often, were the most important relationships to have. The more weak ties you had, the easier it was to find a job.

Later on this research started to bleed into the study of organizations, with people touting the benefits of weak ties even within companies. Other researchers, such as David Krackhardt, fired back with their own research, showing that in many cases weak ties in fact led to poorer performance. Krackhardt studied a firm that sold computer systems to business clients. He asked employees to fill out surveys about their different networks: who their friends were, who they went to for advice, and so on. It turned out that people who had very cohesive networks, especially networks where people were both friends and were relied on for advice, had much higher performance than those with weak ties.

The debate is by no means settled, but the pros and cons on both sides mean that people need a way to understand how the balance should shift in different companies. Different circumstances call for different patterns of interaction, but precisely defining when and how to shift the balance isn't possible with surveys. It is possible, however, with Sociometric Badges. These badges can shed light on exactly how organizational initiatives, such as the all-important purchase of water coolers, play into these different types of networks.

Blue-Collar versus White-Collar Water Coolers

Understanding why the water-cooler effect is important is easy in creative industries. People in these fields intuitively recognize that interaction matters. That's why companies such as Google spend millions on creating a company culture that promotes collaboration and exploration.

The same cannot be said for blue-collar industries. Their mentality hasn't changed much from the days of the industrial revolution, with a focus squarely on efficiency and time management. Efficiency is very different from productivity. Conceptually, increasing productivity by 5% increases the size of the whole pie by 5%. When increasing efficiency by 5%, the size of the pie stays the same, but the slice of the pie devoted to worker pay shrinks by 5%. This increase is often much less valuable than increasing the size of the pie.

The reasoning for a focus on efficiency is that there is an assumption that people in certain jobs can't really be more productive. Packing workers are a prime example of this. Let's assume people are stuffing boxes as fast as they can, and on an average day an average worker can churn out 100 packed boxes. Let's say I discover a new way for people to pack boxes, and now the average worker can pack 105 boxes in a day. If the company only has to pack 105,000 boxes a day, then instead of 1,050 workers, the company would only need 1,000 workers to pack boxes.

Call centers work in a similar way. In a modern call center, often a few thousand employees sit in one huge room answering calls from customers. The company wants employees to answer the greatest number of calls in the least amount of time possible. If it takes you less time to answer a call, then the company can hire fewer staff and become more efficient in general.

So how do you figure out how to answer calls more quickly? For a long time a lot of companies tried to solve this from the top down. Executives and managers would listen in on calls and work out strategies that could be disseminated to the rest of the organization. This method was okay, except that sifting through the millions of calls employees were making to discover successful strategies was often very hard. After all, you can't just organize calls by completion time. A problem that is inherently hard will take longer to complete than a call that involves an easier-to-solve issue. So, by trial and error, people sift through this data and sometimes come out with valuable insight. Other times they're left empty-handed.

As this practice indicates, call center management has not changed much since the 1960s. Call centers back then were organized a lot like small factories. They had about 100 people on the phones organized into teams of about 20 people, normally based on different specialties. When one person on a team was on a break, either for lunch or for a coffee break, no one else could be on a break. The reason was fairly straightforward: If 20 people went on a break at lunch, keeping up with demand would be impossible.

Fast forward to today. Now with thousands of employees, modern call centers no longer necessarily have to choose between call load and team break times. However, that's the way things have been done for decades, and there's no real incentive to change—or so everyone has been led to believe.

Banking on Change

Before diving into how my research group from MIT worked on this problem, I want you to imagine what working in a banking call center is like. You get in at 8:30, put on your headset, and immediately start answering calls. The first person who calls you yells so loud into the headset that you have to turn the volume down. His credit card just got denied, and how can you people run a business like this? He has thousands of dollars left before his limit! You apologize calmly and start looking into it, and for five minutes nothing but vitriol pours through the headset—and this goes on call after call after call.

Working in such a call center is stressful—monumentally so. Your entire day is people yelling at you for stuff that's not your fault. When you finally go on break, no one you know is taking their break. There's just a total lack of social support. It's no wonder that turnover in call centers is 40% per year.

Turnover isn't just a problem for the people who leave and have to find another job. It is psychologically draining to the employees who remain, because seeing your colleagues burn out and quit leaves you with one less person to talk to, one less person to go to for advice. Monetary effects follow as well. Every time a veteran employee leaves, the call center needs to spend months getting a new person up to speed. Not just on formal procedures such as how to answer the phone and how to use the computer system, but also acclimatizing the person to the culture of the organization (see Chapter 2). So not only is working at a call center psychologically difficult, but employees constantly head for the door, deflating morale and adding enormous cost to the company. Typically, companies spend 25% of a veteran's yearly salary to hire and train a replacement.[2] All of a sudden, the toll this environment takes on workers has real economic significance.

One reason we know how much this costs down to the dollar is that call centers are some of the most quantified organizations on the planet. Call center managers measure how quickly people complete calls, how many times they put people on hold, how many mouse clicks employees use during a call, and they even record call content to analyze what went right or wrong. Employee breaks are similarly measured and planned. Precise breaks are allocated to individual employees to ensure maximum uptime on the phones while complying with federal work standards.

The issue of breaks is interesting because in the modern company they have traditionally been viewed with disdain or at least passive disapproval. In many companies, always looking busy is important. Not surprisingly, taking a break to schmooze by the coffee machine or water cooler can lead to negative assessments by coworkers. The common impression is that even the appearance of talking to a colleague about non–work-related activities means that you don't care about your job and must not be working hard enough. This perception turns the coffee area into a barren wasteland, perfectly clean, perfectly stocked, and completely free of socialization.

I've been to many companies where eating lunch at your desk was standard practice. Rather than communicate with coworkers, people felt more comfortable surfing the web and looking at cat videos on YouTube while slurping last night's leftovers. Not that looking at cat videos isn't hypnotic and fun once in a while, but I haven't yet seen a study that proves that extended cat video viewing is correlated with higher productivity.

Lunch is one of the most important times of the day, not only to physically recharge our batteries but also to take some time to network and communicate with others. This idea has been explored in depth in books such as *Never Eat Lunch Alone* by Keith Ferrazzi, which details how people who eat lunch with others advance faster in their careers and perform better in general.

Although to some having lunch with others might be viewed as an additional burden and detract from a much-needed physical break, this strategy ignores a perfect socialization opportunity. For those of us who simply can't make it through the day without reading a bit of trashy news or something else distracting on the web, taking that break separately from lunch is best. You can then preserve your opportunity for socialization but also take some time for yourself.

Both of these activities are part of your work. Communicating with others is work, as is resting your body. The benefits of both have been tangibly demonstrated time and time again, although mostly in the blue-collar workforce. Even at the height of the industrial revolution, when factory workers could be thought of quite literally as cogs in a machine, they still took breaks. Even Taylorist (see Chapter 2) managers who maintained strict work plans and provided only a few minutes each day for breaks realized that workers were much more productive if they had time to eat and take care of biological necessities. This cold, hard reality forced the hands of these calculating factory owners, and this influence is still felt today.

An interesting study on the benefits of breaks took place in a meat packing plant in the U.S. Initially, this factory implemented standard lunchtime and bathroom breaks for its employees. Like call centers, breaks were staggered so that no one on a team would be on a break at the same time. Unfortunately, turnover and fatigue concerns plagued this plant. Researchers showed that creating breaks that were long enough to provide for cohesive interactions significantly reduced employee stress and might help stem the tide of defections and re-energize the workforce.[3] Other research on factory rest periods devised a cryptic name for this kind of break: "Banana Time."

Peanut Butter Jelly Time

The principle behind Banana Time was simple. Workers in factories undergo a ton of physical stress, but they also have a lot of time to think. Working in a meat packing plant can be a very mechanical activity; after you get into a rhythm, breaking out and experimenting with new ways of working can be hard. After all, if you can pack 200 boxes an hour and you went down to packing 50 boxes an hour while trying a new method, your paycheck would suffer. What if you were able to learn from the way other people were working, and you could copy their success and discuss new strategies?

The exchange of work-related information is a second direct benefit of breaks. Beyond the physical respite a break provides, it can also create a platform for ideas. People who have the same job but otherwise don't communicate have the opportunity to compare notes at a high level. Technical terms that might be missed by those not on the front line can be freely exchanged during these breaks. No translation is needed because these people represent a cohesive group of workers.

This type of interaction is fundamentally different from a meeting, which filters ideas through management's idealized view of work. Much like the Toyota production system provided through formal channels, breaks create an opportunity for front-line employee feedback to spread through informal channels. In the original Banana Time study,[4] information sharing during breaks allowed new techniques to percolate through the worker network until these practices were recognized at the company level. These bottom-up innovations were then integrated into training programs and the standard processes of the company.

A complementary third benefit of breaks addresses the mental fatigue associated with these jobs. Previously, workers did not have the opportunity to vent to coworkers or socially support their colleagues. They were alone on the packing floor, grinding away for hour after hour, alone with their thoughts. This by itself can be quite taxing, because staring at raw meat for an entire day can do things to one's appetite, not to mention one's state of mind. Throw in personal problems at home or other things eating away at you, and one can easily see the strong negative impact on productivity and mental health.

On a break these topics are open for discussion. Rather than have to bear all of this stress and physical toil alone, people can complain to coworkers and vent a little steam, or bring up personal issues that have been weighing on their mind and ask for advice. The alternative is to let these problems fester, to let stress at work and at home build up until it's unbearable. Like a pressure cooker left on the stove, it's only a matter of time before this situation explodes, causing people to quit and remove themselves from the whole situation.

These personal discussions go hand in hand with work-related conversations. One is not necessarily more important than the other, but both types of conversations have tangible benefits. Work-related discussions transfer relevant information between employees and can lead to new innovations. Social conversations create trust, build rapport, and relieve stress.

At different times one or the other type of conversation can be more effective. If deadlines are looming and there's pressure to deliver results, sharing work-related information is probably more helpful. If workloads are piling up or it's a particularly stressful time, then social conversations will be more useful. By mixing and matching these conversations appropriately, people can achieve powerful results.

This makes it all the more puzzling that in spite of these benefits many companies have been pushing to reduce breaks. This is especially true in blue-collar work, where companies stick to government-mandated minimums and make sure employees know that they're on the clock whenever they're not doing physical labor. This mirrors the trend in white-collar work discussed earlier, but with the much higher probability of burnout in physically demanding, high-stress roles.

Interestingly, in call centers in particular, some people view turnover as a feature rather than a bug. This view treats people as replaceable cogs in the call center machine and argues that performance degrades over time, and therefore companies shouldn't worry about people burning out. This perspective was laid out in a study by Catriona Wallace from the University of New South Wales,[5] which showed that at one particular call center, productivity was negatively associated with tenure.

Without getting too much into the specifics, the idea is that people work less effectively as their stress increases. As already discussed, call centers are inherently stressful workplaces. Rather than attempt to devise policies to reduce this stress, under this "burn-out" strategy companies merely need to calculate when the loss in productivity due to stress becomes greater than the cost to train a new employee. At that point, it's time to either get rid of that employee or crank up his workload to make it very likely that he'll quit.

This calculation makes a number of assumptions about call centers and businesses in general that seem suspect. First think about how a call center employee would react to being treated this way by an organization. He would immediately realize that there isn't a future for him in this company beyond a year of employment. Although that's not necessarily something to thumb one's nose at, it certainly affects how an employee will interact with a customer. Without the prospect of a continuing career or advancement, why would anyone go the extra mile for a customer? Simply keeping his head down and trying to deal with a difficult call by minimizing the time that he spends on it is much better than actually trying to solve the problem. This tactic decreases the time he spends on the phone, but it would have a huge negative impact on the customer experience and would very quickly start eroding a company's customer base.

On top of this reduction in customer satisfaction, there would be far-reaching effects on morale. When everyone an employee knows is being chewed out and treated poorly by the company, he will start to think pretty quickly about changing jobs. Eventually this toxic environment would lead to an acceleration in turnover, forcing the company to rotate in new employees faster and further increasing costs. Wallace assumes that these employees are low-skilled enough to not have many job prospects, implying that they would stick it out at a job they hate rather than look for other employment. This premise might be right up to a point, but at the very least, people would start looking for other positions almost immediately. Because a fraction of these people would be able to find at least some work, turnover is bound to increase.

When these employees walk out the door, not only do they take with them their individual contributions, but also the tacit knowledge that they acquired about how to do their job effectively. These are the little tricks about work that make things just a bit easier, the pieces of knowledge that slowly spread across a workplace. These tricks could be something as simple as how to circumvent a laborious part of a software program or as nuanced as how to deal with enraged customers screaming at the other end of a phone line. If employees are turned over too quickly, not only do they have less time to uncover these tricks, but a much shorter window exists in which they can share this acquired knowledge. Again, this turnover would exert strong downward pressure on performance across the whole call center operation.

Lastly, and very significantly, turning over employees quickly means that the company sheds any potential future leaders before they even get started moving up the ladder. CEOs from companies as storied as McDonald's, Goldman Sachs, and General Electric started in entry-level positions, rising through the ranks to become the captain of the ship. So not only are companies throwing away organizational performance in the mid-term, but in the long term as well.

Break Value

To many companies, arguing about the value of breaks is a nonstarter. They have been trained over decades to view performance and work as something that happens at a desk, and no amount of subjective arguments will sway their stance. To change this mindset, and that of the business world as a whole, tangible evidence is needed.

This evidence is something that call center employees in particular have been searching for. How could they demonstrate to their employers that they should be able to take breaks with other people? Most of these workers understand all too well the stress of their jobs, and realize that if they don't have tools to deal with it effectively, they will end up burned out and be forced to quit. The conditions were ripe for a project with the Sociometric Badges.

My MIT colleagues and I were approached by Bank of America (BoA) to study precisely this problem of burnout and call center performance. BoA had an interesting issue related to call centers. For some background, note that this company has one of the largest financial call center operations in the country, with thousands of employees stationed at call centers across the United States at all hours of the day.

As in other companies, BoA standardized its call center operation. Its call center in Rhode Island had roughly the same org structure as one in California, the same IT systems, and the same training programs. Employee demographics were also quite similar, with most having high school diplomas and a few with college degrees. Everything that could formally be put into place was the same—and yet, performance was different. Despite all of the similarities between employees in different locations, something about these call centers couldn't be quantified with other methods.

The one possible cause of these differences in performance was culture. Some of these call centers must have different collaboration styles, different cultures, that cause them to be more or less productive. However, there isn't a general understanding of what the term *culture* actually means quantitatively.

The study took place at one of Bank of America's call centers. Our goal was to measure how people interacted and behaved to understand what was making people successful. These call centers typically have thousands of individuals, so instead of looking at everyone, we focused on a few of these teams. By concentrating on the differences across these groups in depth, we hoped to derive general lessons about productivity that could be disseminated across the company.

Notice that I haven't mentioned anything about breaks in this study. From Bank of America's perspective, breaks were not necessarily a consideration. Remember that call centers have been managed one way for more than half a century, and there wasn't a feeling that changes in this age-old break structure would bring any lasting effects. However, BoA knew that something with this traditional model was amiss.

To study these teams in detail, we collected not only badge data, but also performance metrics, demographic information, survey data, and e-mail records.

The performance metrics were relatively simple. Essentially, an employee's performance boils down to how quickly she completes calls on average. In the past some clever people had figured out that they could improve their metrics by hanging up on a customer right at the beginning (or middle) of a call. This would look like a short call from the company's perspective, and so would improve your overall performance numbers. These calls were naturally removed from any calculation of performance for the purposes of the study.

The demographic information we collected was also fairly basic: tenure at the company, gender, age, and a few other features. This information was collected mainly to identify whether any aspect or combination of aspects of particular individuals might lead them to behave in a certain way. For example, you might expect that someone who had been at BoA for a long period of time would have a more tightly knit group of friends than someone who had been there for only a year.

These differences could be further explored with the survey data. Each year employees were surveyed by Bank of America about their stress levels, communication with managers and coworkers, and their overall perception of the company. Stress levels are particularly important at call centers because high stress is a precursor to turnover. If the bank noticed a particular team had higher stress levels than others, it would try to investigate the causes further. For our purposes, this stress data enabled us to investigate behavioral patterns that help mitigate these effects.

In addition to all of this data, we had a few other critical pieces of information. We knew when people took their breaks and when they got lunch. This was important because it enabled us to see what was actually going on during those break periods. Who were people talking to? What were they doing? By combining these different data sources, we were able to get to the heart of the problem: What is it that makes people effective?

Study Setup

The study itself was composed of about 80 people across four teams at one of Bank of America's call centers. We collected data in four-week stages, because in our experience two weeks is roughly one "cycle" of behavior, and there are fairly stable dynamics at the four-week mark. These cycles occur because every so often people go on vacation or take off sick. When the people you communicate with aren't around, it naturally has powerful effects on the way you interact with others. Random external events can also impact behavior, such as a major sporting event or an international crisis. These events can significantly change people's behavior on a particular day. For example, they can spend the first hour of the day talking about the Super Bowl or a natural disaster in another country.

The groups studied were located in different areas of the call center, which itself was basically a huge single room with rows of cubicles for the roughly 3,000 employees that manned the phones. Some variation existed in this physical layout, however. One of the groups had cubicle walls that were below eye level and desks that were about one meter longer than other groups. The other three groups all had high cubicle walls that completely blocked their view of the other people on their team.

When we introduced the badges to participants, management had some trepidation as to what the reaction of employees would be. In particular, the potential perception of the badges as a "big brother" intervention was a concern. After presenting the study plan and the technology, however, we got an extremely positive response. For years employees had tried to convince their managers that their interactions with other workers were important, but they had been unable to tangibly demonstrate the benefits. They felt that this was a huge opportunity for them to show that value.

Bank of America was also focused on showing value. Although they were interested in understanding what unseen aspects of call center culture were responsible for performance differences, the company was more interested in improving them. They wanted to identify specific changes they could make to the way that their people worked and measure the effects of those changes.

This study took place in three phases: The first phase consisted of the initial measurement of the call center teams. After analyzing the data, we would propose and implement changes in work processes at the call center. The second phase was a normalization period of three months, where we would wait for the changes we implemented to become part of the regular process. The last phase was a re-measurement, where we would precisely gauge the behavioral and productivity effects of these changes.

You might ask why the second phase was needed. After all, the impact of a substantive change in the way people work should manifest itself almost immediately after implementation. Everyone has experienced this type of effect at one time or another. A good example is the transition from elementary school to middle school. Although most students aren't able to adjust to this transition immediately, after a few months they settle back into a state of normalcy.

Although behavioral dynamics such as movement and interaction patterns do tend to settle down, other changes can easily upset these dynamics. A major cause for disturbance happens when people are observed. This is experienced by many of us when we take our first driving test. The tester gets in the car with you, and all of a sudden your awareness changes. You might get nervous or suddenly forget months of parallel parking practice, and all because you're being observed.

This phenomenon is known as the *Hawthorne effect*. This effect was formally identified in the early 1930s by researchers studying the Hawthorne Works factory in Cicero, Illinois.[6] These researchers wanted to understand the effect of light levels on employee performance. They designed an elegant study where they would subtly change lighting levels each day and gauge the impact. At first they made the factory floor brighter, observing that performance went up very significantly. Next they turned the lights down, expecting to see a drop in productivity. Instead, they saw the exact same uptick.

Researchers were initially puzzled over these results. Then they hit upon the truth: The workers knew they were being observed, so they endeavored to work harder no matter the change.

In our Bank of America call center study, the three-month break period was put in place to avoid placing emphasis on any initial reaction the employees would have. Three months later, any change we made would have become normal practice. This would enable us to measure the actual effect of our intervention.

With this structure in place, we had only one small hurdle in front of us: deploying the badges.

Deployment

You can't just roll into a company with sensors like the badges and say: "Here, wear this." Most people, including me, just wouldn't feel too comfortable putting on an unknown device that recorded "something" about our behavior.

With that in mind we visited this call center in the suburbs of a mid-size New England city. Standing up front were the badge team from MIT: myself, Taemie Kim, and Daniel Olguin. We were quite the international team, with each of us from a different country— the U.S, South Korea, and Mexico, respectively. People filed into the meeting room where we would present our plan for this project, and their eyes strayed curiously to the small box hanging around our necks.

We explained how this project would work. In a few weeks, we would give everyone who chose to participate a Sociometric Badge, but anyone who didn't want to participate could wear a fake badge that wouldn't collect any data. As far as what data the badge collected, we described the different sensors and their functionality in detail. They could also find a description on the consent forms that we handed out, required by MIT's internal review board to ensure that people understand what they're agreeing to. No individual data would be shown to managers, and their names wouldn't be directly tied to the data collected on the badges.

When we returned, we had to set up the office for data collection. The wearable badge itself is quite easy to use. You simply flip the power switch and hang the badge around your neck. At night, you take off the badge, flip the power off, and plug it into a USB charger. To recognize location, however, we had to put base stations up around the office.

A base station is essentially a wearable badge attached to the wall. Every 10 seconds the base station sends out a ping over Bluetooth. When a wearable badge receives that ping, it can estimate the distance from the base station. By receiving pings from multiple base stations, we can triangulate the signal to figure out where someone is to within about one meter. In order to make these calculations, a researcher has to take a wearable badge and stand in different locations for a few minutes, measuring changes in the signal strength from the different base stations. This is essentially the same way that phone navigation programs work, using Wi-Fi access points instead of Bluetooth.

With the call center thoroughly badged up and prepared, the data collection could begin.

First Results

In the first phase we collected thousands of hours of badge data, tens of thousands of e-mails, and a plethora of productivity data. With this incredibly rich dataset, we could drill down to the millisecond level and understand the context of the behavior we were observing. At first we decided to look at broad trends and see what behaviors were predictive of important outcomes.

Examining the e-mail data, we saw something that at first was almost too perfect to believe. When we plotted the network of e-mail communication between participants, what we saw was almost link-for-link a mirror image of the org chart. There was practically no communication between peers who were on the phones with customers, or for that matter even team managers. All the real communication, if it was happening at all, was happening face to face.

This observation probably shouldn't have been too surprising. E-mail is good for communicating rote information, and so what we were observing was top-down dissemination of simple directives to the front-line employees. To exchange tips on how to deal with customers or to vent about difficult calls, e-mail isn't the appropriate communication medium.

Obviously, this result has implications for the future of call centers. Many companies, including BoA, have placed large bets on a distributed call center workforce. Buying desks and computers for employees, setting up a secure connection at their house, and letting them work from home is easy enough. With no commute for employees and no expensive office space for the company, this would seem at its face to be an ideal solution. The results from the study, however, indicate that if there is any value in communication between employees, the IT tools that are typically available to call center workers are woefully inadequate.

So what about face-to-face interaction? This was, relatively, a much more active communication channel. Employees on the phones interacted with three other employees on average (actually 3.06), and these were almost exclusively other people on their team.

This data became more interesting when we mashed it up with performance and stress data. As far as general statistics are concerned, on average it took employees 263 seconds to resolve a customer call, only a shade over four minutes. Given my personal experience (and frustration) contacting call centers, this seemed exemplary, but the picture was not all rosy. Employees were under a moderate amount of stress, with the average stress rating coming out to 3.07 on a scale from 1 to 5. This might not sound too bad, until you realize that this is their level of stress *all the time*. We expected a result like this given the high turnover typical in call centers, but these numbers point to the substantial problems affecting these workers.

We then got around to testing our hypothesis and correlating these different data sources. Given the numerous arguments listed previously, we expected cohesion to be positively related to productivity and to be associated with reduced stress. Our hypothesis was not only confirmed, it found that cohesion was far and away the single most important factor in regards to productivity and stress.

This point is difficult to understate. To get a sense for the magnitude of the importance of cohesion in worker productivity, cohesion was about 30 times more important than experience. Put another way, having a network that's 10% more cohesive is equivalent to having an additional 30 years under your belt at a call center.

However, these positive benefits weren't confined to productivity alone. Cohesion was strongly related to lower stress levels, albeit not to the degree that we observed with productivity. That being said, high cohesion was responsible for reducing stress by around 6%. Clearly, it is a useful weapon in the war against burnout and mental fatigue.

We examined other factors as well: total amount of face-to-face interaction, network centrality, degree, and so on. However, none of these features were significantly predictive. This seems to be a story about the positive effects of cohesion. The question was: Where did this cohesion come from and how can BoA increase it?

We had to devise a strategy to distinguish interactions that increased cohesion from those that decreased it. Essentially, our program went over each interaction and measured what the effect of removing that interaction from the network would have on the overall cohesion level. We then overlaid these interactions with location and time information to see what places were hotbeds of cohesive interaction. By looking at this "heat map" of interactions and varying it over time, we were able to investigate what activities were actually leading to these important conversations.

The results couldn't have been clearer. Neither formal meetings nor people chatting at their desks encouraged higher cohesion. The vast majority of these interactions were happening away from the desks, during the brief periods of overlap between the lunch breaks of employees on the same team.

This was completely counter to the management dogma on call center operations. The story had continuously been one of efficiency, of aligning work schedules, of reducing interaction. But we had brought hard, objective data to this problem, and had uncovered the harsh reality that people were just doing it wrong. To run the best call center organization, a company needed to encourage cohesion, and to do that it had to align breaks.

After the results of this first phase were shown to managers, they were floored. Mostly they lamented all that the company had lost by managing these groups in the traditional style for so long without checking their assumptions. Still, we needed to test whether or not this was a causal relationship. We needed to move into the second phase, giving people on teams breaks at the same time and observing the results.

Give Me a Break

We changed the break structure for the teams we studied so people on the same team all had the same 15-minute coffee breaks during the day. That was it. Although we shared the results of the study with the teams, we didn't tell them who they had to talk to during these breaks. Our assumption was that if you're on a break with your team, you'll probably talk with the people that you normally talk to. This would by definition increase the cohesion of your network. Rather than forcing people to do something, we're setting up the environment in such a way that they will naturally interact in a way that will make them more effective.

From the bank's perspective, this intervention was free. It wasn't giving employees more breaks, just shifting when they took a break. Because the company has thousands of other call center employees, shifting the load to other teams was fairly straightforward. This made it easier to convince BoA that aligning breaks was the right thing to do. Now all we had to do was wait three months to see the effects.

Final Results—Breaking News

It was not without trepidation that we returned to the call center three months later to see what had happened. Did anything actually change? Were people interacting with their core group during breaks, or did they just bring coffee back to their desks and drink their java in solitude?

Few personnel changes occurred in the intervening period. Some people had left BoA, but overall the group remained more or less the same. We did note that the groups we had studied had low turnover. Over a three-month period, only about 3% of people had left the company, implying that the turnover rate on a yearly basis would be 12%, drastically lower than the 40% industry average.

This result was encouraging, and lent us confidence as we handed out badges for the final phase of this project. We were going to collect data for another four weeks, and at the end of it, we would have a definitive answer. Do breaks really make people more effective?

The results were clear-cut. Cohesion was up by 18% in the third phase, an extremely significant result. This is like adding 50 years of experience to each employee, a truly astronomical number. These teams had become far more cohesive than they were before, but at a certain level this result isn't surprising. We had set up the environment so that this was almost bound to happen.

The impact on the bottom line was equally powerful. The performance increases associated with this intervention would conservatively yield $15 million in yearly savings on call center costs across BoA. Changing how people spent 15 minutes of their day yielded $15 million.

This result is truly astonishing. When we talk about performance gains of this magnitude, increasing performance by double-digit percentages, the normal reaction from companies is "Wow, we have to change everything to achieve that kind of growth." What these results show, however, is that companies don't need to think about these massive changes to achieve huge gains. If instead they can find the social levers that people are responsive to, and act on them in the right way, they are going to get big results.

Overall, the study showed definitively that breaks matter as a way to increase cohesion. Not only do they matter, but they're also crucial to the effectiveness of companies in general and call centers in particular. Rather than thinking of information exchange and social support as something that only matters in the most creative and high-level jobs, this study shows that it matters even in organizations as seemingly straightforward as call centers.

So what's the most important place in the office? It's not your desk or the CEO's office or a meeting room. It's the simple, inconspicuous water cooler.

4

The Death of Distance?
Measuring the Power of Proximity

With companies not just to a single location, but more and more frequently spread across the globe, how much does having a water cooler (see Chapter 3) really matter today? It's not hard to imagine that the water cooler effect will gradually fade in importance as workforces become more and more distributed and as technologies allow workers to collaborate more effectively across huge distances.

The revolution in communication technologies continues, slowly lowering the barriers to remote work. From e-mail to instant messaging to video conferencing, each has served to make collaboration over distance much easier than in the past.

For decades these communication technologies did not fundamentally change the way that people worked. Yes, now companies could have branches in different locations, and as an employee, you might be working with someone whom you didn't meet face to face, but you were still going to work in an office. You still commuted to work and had coworkers who were physically in the same place as you. In the 1970s, however, this model started to shift.

The term *telecommuting* was first coined in 1973 and encapsulated this change in work. Information technology had advanced to a point where some people could do their job from home part of the time. Particularly for people working in computer-intensive jobs such as software development or even factory management positions, telecommuting can be an attractive option.

One of the main benefits of telecommuting is that workers are able to balance their personal and professional responsibilities. If your child is sick and has to stay home from school, for example, tele-commuting gives you the ability to work from home and take care of your child at the same time. As any working parent can attest, this benefit offers substantial relief from the frantic scrambling to find a babysitter that typically occurs in this situation.

Telecommuting was originally conceived as an occasional perk. If sometimes you needed to work from home, you could feel free to work a few days a month in your pajamas. Over the following decades, however, this model also started to change. Instead of people staying at home one day a week, this gradually stretched to two days, then three. Eventually, some organizations found it desirable to have peo-ple telecommute every day.

One of the places where telecommuting first manifested itself was call centers. In call centers, having employees talk to each other was never thought to be important, so having people work from home was a logical step. Physical space could be reserved for someone else.

Telecommuting also began to expand over time. Rather than hav-ing individual workers opt into these programs, companies began closing down entire offices and making whole branches of the com-pany virtual. Now some companies just need to pay for an employee's Internet connection and office supplies. There are no leases to sign, no cleaning crews to hire. The reduction in employee commuting times also meant that people could spend more time with their family and even more time working if they so chose.

This change hasn't been confined to call centers. Organizations in nearly every sector are embracing what are being called "virtual orga-nizations." Two guiding principles of these organizations are effi-ciency and flexibility. The idea is that these organizations are efficient because moving physical bodies around wastes a lot of stuff: time, fossil fuels, and the monetary cost of maintaining a physical office. The average American spends about 50 minutes per day commuting. Splitting that time evenly between family and work would enable peo-ple to spend 5% more time working—not an insignificant number.

These organizations can also be more flexible because telecom-muting employees are able to choose whom they spend time with. Because they can't bump into people in the hallway or be roped into lunch with coworkers, they can't be randomly "interrupted." Instead they have to rely on e-mail, the phone, and tools such as Skype to talk to other people. All of these tools are used in a completely intentional way, so telecommuters can set up meetings and calls only with those people with whom they absolutely need to communicate.

An interesting parallel to the telecommuting trend is *offshoring*. Offshoring generally involves taking a part of a company and placing it in another country, typically one where the cost of living is far lower than in the original location. Classic examples of this trend include transplanting call centers from the U.S. to India or moving software development to eastern Europe. Although these offshored divisions usually need to interact quite frequently with their onshore counterparts, the rise of remote collaboration technology has made offshoring a much more palatable option for business leaders.

The decision to offshore an operation is nearly always based on economic considerations. As education levels in the developing world have caught up to more traditionally advanced countries, there is no longer a strong concern about a drop in production quality due to unskilled workers. In fact, because people in developing countries often have to deal creatively with challenging problems, their location can actually contribute to greater innovation.

An intriguing example of this phenomenon comes from the Nirma Institute of Technology in India. In the early 2000s, students in the computer science department of that university wanted to do research on virtual reality. Unfortunately, even the least expensive virtual reality gloves cost hundreds of dollars. This was well out of reach for the vast majority of students at the time. They had to develop a lower cost alternative to perform their work.

Playing around with a computer mouse, they hit upon the idea of attaching multiple mice together into a glove-like contraption. A string would attach to each finger, which would then attach to a mouse wheel. Bending the fingers in a particular direction would cause a corresponding movement of the mouse wheel, which would be fed to the computer. In that way the students were able to create an extremely accurate substitute for a virtual reality glove for around $20.

Companies look at examples of this kind of ingenuity and realize that if they can get one of these students to work for their company at half the cost, they are probably getting a good deal. As this trend accelerates, suddenly companies are no longer considering offshoring one part of an organization but many. Most major organizations have operations on multiple continents and dozens of countries. IBM, for example, operates in more than 170 countries. Given that as of 2012 approximately 195 countries exist, IBM is about as "global" an organization as you can get. Most companies that make extensive use of remote workers and offshoring, however, don't look at the results of these changes beyond the immediate impact on their personnel costs. In order to determine the real effect of these practices, you to need to look at some hard data.

So, Should I Stay at Home and Work in My Pajamas?

The question on many people's minds is, "Should I stay at home and work in my pajamas?" I'm not exactly a morning person myself, and I have to say the temptation to walk around my house in slippers sipping hot cocoa is pretty strong. Besides a significant increase in cocoa consumption and the ensuing increase in my waistline, what's the downside?

First, let's talk about telecommuting. It represents a flexible kind of workplace, where you only stay home when going to work is very inconvenient. In general, few downsides exist for this arrangement. Sure, you might miss a few interactions at work, but from that perspective, a day at home telecommuting is essentially equivalent to taking one day of vacation. Ample evidence shows that vacation and recharging in general are good for worker performance, and if you had to go to work knowing you had five hours of errands ahead of you when you got home, you probably wouldn't be very effective.

Ideally, however, telecommuting should be used somewhat infrequently. The principle behind telecommuting is that you can work from home when necessary, but you're still coming into the workplace the vast majority of the time. By contrast, when people only work from home, they are completely cut off from the physical workplace.

Let's consider the case where you're the only person working from home while the rest of your colleagues continue to go to the office. The time your colleagues would have spent interacting with you face to face is reallocated to

- Interacting with other people
- Communicating with you via other channels

The main interactions that are lost are social in nature: the bumping into other people and the schmoozing that happens before and after meetings. Because they're not strictly work related, these interactions are much less likely to be continued after someone becomes a remote worker. Communication that is necessary to complete specific tasks, however, shifts to e-mail, phone, and video chat.

So how does telecommuting impact individual performance? Let's look at the numbers. In the call center study from Chapter 3, my team and I were able to measure the effects of face-to-face interaction, and we also collected e-mail data. E-mail was a perfect representation of the org chart. In other words, peers didn't communicate with each other electronically, and e-mail communication in general had no correlation with performance. Removing face-to-face interaction and cohesion from consideration in our model of productivity leaves an average call handle time of 297 seconds.

The average call handle time in the original dataset was 263 seconds, which implies that if we completely eliminated face-to-face interaction for an individual call center employee, we would expect performance to decrease by 12.9%. This is an incredibly significant effect. If we sent all call center employees home, we would have to hire 12.9% more people to handle the same call volume. At an average salary in the U.S. of around $30,000, in a call center operation such as Bank of America's with more than 10,000 call center employees, this translates into an additional expense of at least $38 million.

This equation also leaves out the mental toll this action would take on workers. We would expect to see stress increase quickly as well, with a 13.1% increase in stress if we remove face-to-face interaction. Not only would removing this interaction make a hard job even harder, but it would contribute to turnover and further add to the cost of running a call center operation.

These costs have been examined in creative industries as well. For better or for worse, some teams are required to be entirely virtual. If you're trying to run an international advertising campaign, for example, you need people on the ground in many different countries collaborating with each other. In general, these teams are far less effective than co-located teams (teams in the same location). They trust each other less, and completing tasks takes them longer.

Elena Rocco from the University of Michigan designed an ingenious study[1] to test some countermeasures for low distributed team performance. Rather than only study whether face-to-face groups work better than remote groups, Rocco had one experimental condition where people met face to face before going off and working remotely. The idea was that by getting a feel for the other people on your team when you met in person, you would know how to respond to them better and interact on a deeper level when you were no longer co-located.

In her study, face-to-face teams were the highest performers, but they were followed quite closely by teams that met face-to-face first and then worked remotely. Groups that only worked remotely were by far the lowest performers. This study shows that getting everyone together in person before kicking off a project is probably worth the cost of a few plane tickets, even though doing so is not practical in all circumstances.

Offshoring is a different beast altogether. When a company places parts of the organization in separate locations, collaboration within a division is not necessarily the issue. Rather, problems come from coordination between divisions. Language problems can, of course, contribute to these difficulties. At a basic level, if people literally can't speak the same language, then they will find collaboration challenging. Beyond that issue is the potentially acrimonious relationship that can develop between groups who are based in different locations.

Michael O'Leary and Mark Mortensen from MIT explored this problem by examining the configuration of groups that were collaborating in different locations.[2] Specifically, they looked at the number of team members in different sites and saw how this distribution related to team success. Their main hypothesis was that an imbalance in the number of people at different sites could cause individuals to identify as part of different groups, drastically reducing trust and productivity.

One might believe that the evenly balanced or far out-of-balance teams would have the most trouble. After all, two groups of equal size might both want to claim ownership of a project. On the flip side, if one group is vastly bigger than another, you would expect them to run roughshod over the smaller team. What the study found was a different story.

Groups that were relatively even were actually quite productive. Because the teams in different locations were of equal size, they didn't feel threatened by the other group. This enabled them to work out their differences equitably. In the very imbalanced groups, a similar effect was observed. In this case it was never a question of what group was in charge, because the larger group could always override the smaller one. With that issue settled, conflict around project control faded into the background.

The worst teams had one group that was slightly larger than the other group. The minority party knew they were outnumbered, but resented the fact that they could be excluded from the decision process by the larger group. This often degenerated into pointless bickering, which had strong negative effects on performance.

Notice that this discussion doesn't even consider organizational structure. This is simply the number of people in different locations. The takeaway is that beyond the necessities of setting up meetings and creating an org chart that effectively ties in remote workplaces, social considerations have to be accounted for as well. You need to think about how to set up these remote workplaces in such a way that people feel like they're collaborating with each other rather than working at odds.

As discussed earlier in this chapter in the case of creating a virtual organization, meeting face to face before starting work on a project is critical. The same can be said of offshoring. If you want things to go well, if you want people to care about each other and think of themselves as part of the same team, you need at least some team members to meet face to face.

Co-Located Offices: The Gold Standard?

The discussion up to this point has implied that all face-to-face interaction is created equal. The Bank of America call center study (see Chapter 3) showed that's clearly not the case. Later chapters show further support for this idea as well. Different patterns of interaction have different effects on productivity and job satisfaction.

How do companies get the right people to talk to each other, or even get people to talk in the first place? Instead of focusing on using formal meetings to this end, this section looks at how to organize the layout of a workplace to make it more likely that the right people will talk to each other.

It should come as no surprise that you're not equally likely to talk to everyone in the office. After all, some office buildings house tens of thousands of employees. In these skyscrapers, companies can span dozens of floors that themselves can be thousands of square feet. As a matter of common sense, you are not likely to talk to someone 20 floors down from you. Conversely, you should be extremely likely to talk to someone who sits next to you.

Expanding on this theory a bit, the general idea is that the probability that two people will interact is inversely proportional to the distance between their desks. Because you can't walk in a straight line from one desk to another without having to jump over cubicle walls (or through them), the theory takes into account the distance you have to walk from one desk to another. To calculate this distance for our study, we drew lines across corridors and hallways, paying attention to the points of intersection between these different lines. These maps allowed us to automatically calculate the distance between people who sit on the same floor.

Dealing with people on different floors of the same building might seem simple at first. You could just add the vertical distance you need to travel on the elevator to get to the other person's floor. This distance, however, doesn't capture the actual amount of time needed to travel from one floor to another. If you take the elevator, you need to press a button, wait for the elevator to come, get into the elevator, press another button, wait for other people's stops, and then finally get off on the right floor. Although people can take the stairs, the physical effort required often dissuades people from taking them even for a single floor.

These points lead to the conclusion that being on a separate floor is fundamentally different from being on the same floor. Even the difference of a few staircases should have a powerful effect on interaction patterns, one that's slightly different from the concept of distance.

This makes the company campus setup all the more interesting. Company campuses are made up of a number of buildings housing different parts of the organization, all grouped together in a single location. Some campuses can sprawl for miles, whereas others can be smaller and encompass only a few clustered buildings.

Campuses are particularly hot in technology companies, with juggernauts such as Google and Facebook buying hundreds of acres of land to build, in essence, a company city. Google's campus, for example, is replete with beach volleyball courts, bowling alleys, fitness centers, and dozens of cafes and restaurants that serve Googlers some of the finest "cafeteria" food in the world.

These campuses create a strong sense of community. People throughout Google and Facebook eat the same food, go to the same gyms, and play the same games. Beyond being fabulous perks, these shared experiences make relating to each other easier for people in different parts of the organization.

The question is: Do these campuses actually yield better interaction patterns? One of the major reasons companies invest in these campuses is that it's believed they promote closer collaboration between different parts of the company. Although the possibility for interacting face to face technically exists when you're on the same campus, whether people can make use of this co-location to do more than simply organize meetings is an open-ended question.

An issue is that walking between buildings takes an order of magnitude more time than going between floors. You normally have to take two elevators or two sets of stairs in addition to walking across the campus to get to your destination. As such, it is incredibly unlikely that this will lead to serendipitous conversations. Even without looking at the data, one could be quite confident that people in different buildings on campus won't hang out in one another's coffee areas.

That's not to say that serendipity can't happen in company campuses. At company-wide talks or interest group meetings, bumping into someone who sends your thinking in a completely new direction and starts off a new collaboration is entirely possible. Indeed, this serendipity is probably the biggest benefit of company campuses. However, serendipitous interactions are probably not going to happen in the spaces between buildings because you walk with people you already know. This shifts the focus in company campuses from the actual office buildings to the event spaces and central social areas where people from other areas can actually meet.

Companies such as Google get this concept. The company offers a variety of classes and speaking events from outside researchers and personalities that pique the interest of different constituencies at Google, creating many opportunities for division-spanning collaboration to occur. Companies need to take these events into consideration when planning their new campuses. Otherwise, they risk creating a bunch of corporate islands that happen to be in the same pond.

As employees can move around within these campuses and the workforce becomes more mobile, even the one desk per person standard has shifted. The concept of open seating in particular has gained in popularity over the last decade, enabling people to choose their own desk on a daily basis within their team's area. One of the main benefits of such areas is that as collaboration needs change, people are free to rearrange their seats to sit closer to the people they need to talk to.

ESPN is one company that has embraced this model for its video editors. For those who haven't watched ESPN, they run live sports broadcasts and slick analysis and news shows that seamlessly intersperse commentary and event clips. They are a massively successful organization, holding a nearly insurmountable share of the U.S. sports market and commanding huge premiums in terms of cable fees and advertising prices.

While they have huge resources at their disposal, what always interested me about this organization was that they would have clips of some of the most obscure sporting events going on in other parts of the world. When I visited ESPN's headquarters, for example, I saw clips of professional Polish volleyball, African cricket matches, and minor league baseball games. When an interesting play happens in one of these matches, it's not unusual to see it fed to a number of the network's programs to be disseminated to the wider world.

I had always assumed ESPN had people watching major sporting events in the U.S., but I also assumed they were alerted to relevant plays in obscure sports by media partners in other countries. Wrong. ESPN has dozens of video editors, watching every single sporting event that is broadcast anywhere in the world every hour of every day. This means that if you walk into the editing room at 3 a.m. on a Tuesday, you'll find a bunch of editors sitting at their desks watching sports.

The reason that ESPN uses open seating becomes much clearer when taking into account this work style. If many sporting events are going on, then more people need to be sitting around watching sports. For major events, usually multiple people are watching from different angles. Having these people sit near each other is better so they can discuss how interesting a particular play is. Assigning people set desks at different time periods could probably reduce the overall number of seats, but the room would become significantly overcrowded during huge sporting events such as the Olympics or March Madness.

ESPN has even extended this model to their individual television programs. Each team responsible for a television program sits in an assigned area, a small part of a larger bullpen where the producers and editors for the shows are located. The desk areas rotate over time, so that the morning *Sportscenter* crew swaps desks with the 6 p.m. *Sportscenter* staff in the afternoon. Within each seating area, people can just log in to a computer and sit down wherever they want. This capability is particularly important when they need to coordinate with people on other shows. You want to check how the shows before and after you are planning on covering an event so that you make sure storylines aren't repeated ad nauseum and to facilitate unique takes on these events with your colleagues.

Intuition suggests that distance matters, and some of the world's most successful companies are embracing this fact. To discover the levers that really make these distance mechanisms work, however, we need to look at the data.

More Than a Tape Measure

Looking at distance in office environments is in itself a fascinating and fast-growing research field, and has many excellent books devoted to that area of study. A great starting place on this topic would be *The Space-Organisation Relationship* by Kerstin Sailer.

There are many ways to look at distance data, but this discussion simplifies things a bit so that the numbers are easier to understand. In particular, our studies take into account four different distances between people:

- Next to each other
- Same row or hallway
- Same floor (or less than 50 meters apart)
- Different floor (or more than 50 meters apart)

These distances can, of course, be differentiated by counting the number of steps between desks and looking at big scatter plots; but what you'll see is that after you get past the same hallway, the effective probability of interaction drops precipitously.

The following discussion looks at two badge datasets, one from a German bank and another from an IT firm. In these studies we knew exactly where people sat, and for a four-week period we knew who spoke with whom. The next step is to see what fraction of these interactions occurred between people at different distances. Let's go over a simple example.

In Table 4.1, each entry represents how much one person spoke to another. For example, the entry in row B, column A indicates that B spoke with A nine times. In this example, let's say that A and B sit next to each other (distance 1), but C sits in another row (distance 2). Let's group these interactions by distance.

Table 4.1 Quantity of Interaction

Person	A	B	C
A	—	9	1
B	9	—	0
C	1	0	—

As you can see from Table 4.2, in this example people who sit next to each other always talk to each other, but only 1 interaction occurs at distance 2.

Table 4.2 Probability of Interaction

Distance	Interactions	Percentage of Interactions
1	9	90%
2	1	10%

In the German bank study data, we also looked at e-mail communication as it relates to distance. This issue is interesting because e-mail is not bound at all by physical constraints. E-mailing someone sitting next to you takes just as much effort as e-mailing someone on the other side of the world. If e-mail also falls prey to distance effects, however, then the implication is that to spur truly global communication, companies need to rely on other communication channels as well.

Some early work on e-mail communication and distance effects comes out of the University of Toronto. In their study, people in a pharmaceutical company were randomly assigned offices when they joined the company. As a result, people in the same workgroup were now no closer than people from different workgroups. If distance influenced communication probabilities, then it must be due to distance effects rather than formal work needs.

As you might suspect, they found exactly what we are hypothesizing that we'll see with face-to-face communication: the greater the distance between people's desks, the less likely they were to communicate over e-mail.

Now you have a pretty good idea about what we expect to see when we look at this study data. So let's get right to it.

Distance Makes the Heart Grow Fonder?

Figure 4.1 shows the percentage of interactions against the distance between people's desks. Face-to-face interaction was detected using Sociometric Badges, and e-mail data was collected from company servers. Importantly, in the e-mail data we screened out mass e-mails because they don't really capture conversations between people, but rather something more along the lines of shouting through a megaphone.

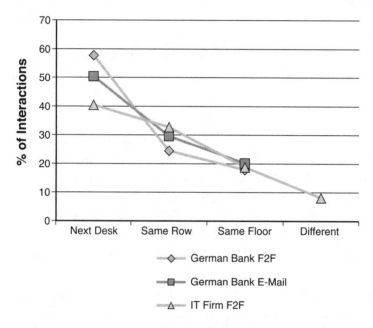

Figure 4.1 Communication-distance breakdown.

Putting the data from both companies on the same graph reveals something interesting: the negative relationship between distance and communication is nearly the same for both organizations, even when we throw e-mail into the mix. These are two very different companies. One has individual engineers in the midwestern United States work on individual tasks, while the other has people working collaboratively on different aspects of financial products in Germany. They have employees from different cultural and educational backgrounds, different organizational goals and formal processes, and yet the distance between desks appears to be one of the main drivers of interaction.

Getting into the specifics, the downward trend observed as distance increases is not surprising given the previous discussion. The likelihood that you'll bump into somebody, the chance that you'll make the extra effort to specifically swing by someone's desk, gets drastically lower as distance between desks increases.

The decrease in e-mail communication, while in line with previous research, is still incredibly fascinating. What makes e-mailing people in different locations so difficult?

To some extent, the difficulty of cold calling explains this phenomenon. Although some naturally outgoing people don't have trouble calling up someone they don't know to ask a question, for many people this task is quite difficult. E-mailing someone you don't know can be just as awkward.

The German bank data allows us to test this theory. With the data, we're able to actually observe how much you e-mail people you spend time with versus people you don't spend time with and detect any differences. If our hypothesis holds, then the amount you e-mail someone should be strongly correlated with how much time you spend with that person.

An analysis of the German bank data provides results that at first seem surprising. In general, the amount an employee e-mails another person is not related at all to how much she talks to him face to face. Remember from the overall relationship between distance and communication probability, however, that the farther away people's desks are from each other, the less likely the two people are to communicate. Taken together, these results imply that people switch off using face-to-face and e-mail to fulfill their communication needs.

Think about this result with a simple example. If I talk to someone a lot face to face, it has no bearing on how much I e-mail that other person. But suppose I need to communicate 10 "bits" of information to that person. Let's say that one face-to-face interaction can transmit 2 bits of information, while e-mail can transmit 1 bit of information. There are many ways that I can get to 10 bits: 5 face-to-face interactions, 10 e-mails, 3 face-to-face interactions and 4 e-mails, and so on.

Now assume that for different people I need a different number of bits. So for Bob I might need 10 bits, whereas for Alice I might need 15 bits. I could choose to mix these bits in different ways, with some bits being filled more by face-to-face communication but other bits being filled more by e-mail communication.

Drilling into the data a bit further provides some insight into how people might make these decisions. For one class of relationships— people who sat next to each other—the study results showed a correlation between e-mail and face-to-face communication. In that case, the amount of e-mail was strongly negatively related to the amount of face-to-face interaction.

This makes a lot of sense because if you sit next to someone, just leaning over and asking him a quick question is easier than sending him an e-mail. As someone gets farther away from your desk, however, the type of information you want to communicate likely plays a role in what communication medium you choose. As discussed in Chapter 3, e-mail is excellent at disseminating easily codifiable information, whereas face-to-face communication is effective for communicating nuanced and complex information.

Long Table, Short Table

Seemingly lost in this discussion is how the actual furniture that populates offices impacts face-to-face interaction. There are many furniture choices in the workplace: cubicles, long desks, wall separators, private offices, and so on. From the previous analysis of distance effects, we can already make some strong predictions.

Long desks increase distance between people, and thus should have a chilling effect on the amount of interaction. Private offices increase distances even further. Smaller cubicles are positive from a distance perspective, but high cubicle walls could potentially make communication more difficult.

The question of desk size in particular is interesting because it seems like such a minor difference. After all, a six-foot-long desk versus a seven-foot-long desk doesn't seem like a big deal.

In our Bank of America project, we were fortunate to have groups that sat at desks of different lengths. One group had longer desks with low cubicle walls, while the others had traditional cubicles with smaller desks. The group with the longer desks had 43% less intra-group communication, while the groups with cubicles were internally very tightly connected.

These effects aren't only limited to desk size. Other seating areas around the office are also strongly impacted by distance. In a study at an online travel company, the size of the lunch tables was a strong predictor of future communication and individual performance.

At this company, people could eat lunch at their desk, in a small café area, or downstairs in the main cafeteria. Obviously eating lunch at your desk meant eating by yourself, while the small café area had tables that could accommodate up to 4 people. The cafeteria, on the other hand, had tables that could fit up to 12 people.

After collecting badge and e-mail data for four weeks, we saw that, not surprisingly, after an employee ate lunch with someone, he was more likely to talk to that person during the rest of the day. Eating lunch together enables people to get a sense for what everyone is working on and what problems they're having. This deep knowledge is crucial if you ever have an issue with your own work because you'll have a strong network spread across a diverse group of areas, making it more likely that you'll know someone who can help you find a solution.

What was interesting, however, was that people who ate lunch in larger groups weren't going to the cafeteria with that entire group. The larger tables forced different groups to sit together, which caused smaller lunch groups to merge into a "super-group." This activity wasn't possible in the café, because the tables were too small.

These larger lunch group interactions directly led to higher group cohesion and consequently to higher performance. People who interacted in these large lunch groups were 36% more likely to interact with each other at some other point in the day compared to other groups, and they were also significantly more resistant to the effects of stressful events such as layoffs.

At the root of these incredible effects, however, was a simple element: a longer lunch table. The decision to buy those tables had a significant impact on this company and its employees. These results led one of my colleagues to suggest: "Maybe we should just duct-tape smaller tables together!"

So, Where Should I Sit?

You might be tempted to think that you should sit in a desk that's in as central a location as possible. After all, according to the results of our study, if you minimize your distance to other people, then you'll maximize the likelihood of communication. This calculation is a little more complicated, though, because as soon as you are farther than one row away from another person, the likelihood that you'll interact nosedives. To talk to the highest number of people, you would actually want to be in as crowded an area as possible.

That assumes, however, that you just want to talk to *a lot* of people, rather than the *right* people. What you should be trying to figure out is whom you should be sitting close to, both for getting your job done and for making good connections.

Companies also need to think about the importance of office layout. Rather than sticking people into open desks just because they're open, managers need to consider the effects on collaboration and attempt to create a layout that makes it easy for the right groups to communicate with each other.

Beyond the layout of the space, furniture choices have effects as well. The size of your desk impacts not just how likely you are to talk to the people sitting next to you, but by extension the probability that you'll interact with people all across the office. Taken to the extreme, this means we should all sit in single chairs next to our colleagues to minimize the distance between us. This underscores the tension between the need to have a desk to get stuff done but also to create an environment where you're closer to the right people. Clearly, employees need some kind of desk in order to work, but maybe it's not the sprawling workspace in a private office that has been an ideal. Figuring out the right balance between desk space and communication requirements is crucial to creating a workplace that fits the needs of employees and the organization.

Office furniture also includes common seating areas and cafes, which have become staples in the modern company. As our results at the online travel company show, the choice of a small, round coffee table versus a large, square lunch table takes on an added, serious dimension. These areas are foci of social activity, and ensuring that they not only look nice, but also have real, tangible benefits for the company is key.

Although the study found that larger lunch tables made people more productive, that will not necessarily be the case in other companies. When sitting down for lunch, you need to ask yourself: What kind of connections do I need to do my job, and what pattern of collaboration will be most supportive for me right now? Rather than sitting with your best friends, maybe branching out one week to sit with a larger group from another department makes sense. This would make talking with those people later in the week easier and would provide a window into other activities around the workplace.

Although in this chapter we've discussed increasing the likelihood of interaction, we can also use this effect to decrease communication between different groups when it's desirable. For example, the accounting division might not need to communicate much with the research division, so managers should try to put more space between these divisions to reduce extraneous communication. Because a workday contains a finite amount of time, spending time wisely and making sure the environment is set up in such a way that employees will naturally talk to the right people are important.

Distance is a natural lever that companies can pull to get predictable responses in collaboration patterns, but it doesn't force people to behave in a specific way. If I want to talk to someone on another floor, I'm perfectly capable of taking the elevator and walking to his or her desk. However, when I'm simply walking around the office and not looking to talk to anyone in particular, I'm much more likely to bump into the people who are close to me. The role of individuals and company leaders is to engineer the environment so that those serendipitous interactions are as useful as possible.

This chapter covered a lot about remote work and telecommuting. A large, robust body of research indicates that companies need to figure out some way to get employees together face to face, because remote work tools just aren't cutting it. The more that employees can meet in person with their team, the more effective they will be and the better the team will perform. When making the decision to work from home, employees must weigh personal needs against the negative impact it will have on their colleagues and on them as individuals.

Although remote work is certainly a reality and will have to continue into the future, people need to pay a lot more attention to communication to make those arrangements work. Face-to-face meetings are an investment, not a cost; the small amount of resources that are put into physical space comes back many-fold in increased productivity and job satisfaction.

Companies should always look to physical space as a key part of their toolbox for changing patterns of collaboration and behavior. The actual layout of the office, the type of furniture, and the decision to let employees work remotely all have a profound impact on both companies' and individuals' success. Distance is not dead. If anything, it's more central to our lives than ever.

5

I'm the Expert

Why Connections Are More
Important Than Test Scores

When I was in the fifth grade, I got blisters on my thumbs. The cause wasn't an overly exhausting rock-climbing expedition or working long hours at the wood shop. No, my blisters were caused by a far grander, nobler endeavor: I was playing video games.

Over the course of the year, I conservatively estimate that I played Nintendo for about 2,000 hours in total, or about 5 hours a day. During this time, my games of choice were *Final Fantasy* and *Contra*. It was while playing the latter that I developed the aforementioned blisters.

Contra is an action game where you control a commando fighting alien hordes. As you progress through a series of levels, you must dodge enemy fire and dispatch said enemies with your own attacks. If you're hit once by any enemy bullet you instantly die, and the fast-paced nature of the game means that to succeed you need to quickly change directions while simultaneously mashing the "fire" button.

After approximately 1,000 hours of playing *Contra*, I had become an expert at this game. I knew exactly how to react to my enemies, and I had learned the strategies for vanquishing the various bosses that appear throughout the game.

I had become the prototypical expert. I had mastered every aspect of a particular (if narrow) field, and I could perform at levels well beyond those of novices and intermediate players.

Throughout our lives we go through similar phases in many different areas, for most of us outside the world of gaming. We go to college and become experts in a field of study, we work for a company and become an expert in a technical area, we get married and become an expert on a particular relationship, and so on. This learning and evolving of our understanding is central to the human experience.

The way organizations have nurtured and helped us refine our expertise, however, has changed drastically over time, mostly due to the ever-increasing complexity of the type of work that we do. As a concrete example, compare a computer programmer posting from 1958[1] and one from 2012:

Computer Program'ers

Help develop large-scale computer-based systems at SDC

As a Programmer at System Development Corporation in Santa Monica, California, you work with Operations Research Scientists and Behavioral Scientists to develop complex computer-centered systems in a number of fields, including air operations.

As these systems are computer-based, programming is an essential function at SDC. Programming is not a service department at SDC.

SDC offer Programmers:

1. A wide range of assignments in the use of computers for simulation and control.

2. An opportunity to work on advanced programming techniques.

3. Advanced facilities, including 704's, 709's, and even more sophisticated computers.

4. A training program in the use of these computers.

One of the more interesting aspects of programming at SDC lies in the variety of data manipulation techniques. Assignments involve inputs such as magnetic tape data, keyed data, radar digital data, punched card data. Outputs include charactron displays, magnetic tape data, data link and teletype.

Positions are open at all levels. The positions call for at least some college math, a minimum of one year's programming experience (although your experience does not need to be on advanced computers) and strong profession interest in programming.

Travel and Moving Allowances to Santa Monica, California

For New York Interview contact Harold Willson at Plaza 3-4800 between 10 AM and 7 PM Monday, Dec. 1 through Thursday, Dec. 4. Collect calls accepted. If you are unable to contact Mr. Wilson while he is in New York, you are invited to send your resume to him at SDC in Santa Monica, California.

System Developm'nt Corporation 2500 Colorado Avenue Santa Monica, California

Although the job description itself looks humorous and quaint today, there are a few things to pay attention to. One is that almost no pre-qualifications are needed for a job that can be incredibly complex. Applicants essentially needed to take a few classes in programming and be interested in the field to qualify. Another is that the specifications even for a senior-level position don't require experience working in this field.

Now look at a recent job listing for an entry-level programming position:

Software Developer - Python - OOP Application Frameworks

SKILLS REQUIRED:

Computer Science, Object-Oriented Application Frameworks, iOS Development, Android Development, Python, OOP, Objective-C, Java, PHP

JOB DESCRIPTION:

Python Software Developer - Object-Oriented Application Frameworks

*This position is located in Santa Cruz! Come work and play

Are you a Jr Software Developer with strong OOP experience and have mobile development experience? If so, we have an amazing opportunity for you to build a strong career in not only the hot mobile industry, but also the hot healthcare industry! You will work closely with the CTO on development of a cross-platform mobile framework, where you can learn tremendously.

Our startup team has tremendous growth potential, but also has the financial backing of our highly successful and established parent company in the medical technology industry.

Our new group is focusing on development of mobile applications that help clinicians improve patient care securely.

What you need for this position:

- Bachelor's in Computer Science or related degree

- Strong with Object Oriented Programming / Object-Oriented Application Frameworks

- Great with Python

Plus if you have programming experience with...

- Objective C and Java

- Mobile Development

What's in it for you:

- Great compensation (salary and equity package)

- Comprehensive benefits

- Significant learning and advancement opportunities

- Casual and collaborative work environment

So, if you are a Software Developer with strong OOP and Python experience, do apply today! This is an immediate fill position!

Must be authorized to work in the United States on a full-time basis for any employer.

From a skills perspective, the recent job posting is incredibly complex. The applicant needs to have trained as an undergraduate for four years to learn this field and have specific experience developing programs using the languages the company uses, which speaks to the larger trend of the increasing need for training and expertise in today's world.

Imagine a programmer from the 1970s going to apply for a position today. He would be quickly shown the door. On the other hand, a programmer from today could easily go back and win a position a few decades ago. Today's novices are yesterday's experts.

This increasing reliance on expertise has caused a shift in the way that organizations and potential hires view their relationship. In exchange for an employee's devotion to a single organization, a company was obligated to train him and nurture his skills until he became an expert in his field. In the past, companies looked to acquire the best people who could learn the skills they needed to succeed, whereas today employers look for people who already have all the skills.

To a large extent, this trend is being driven by societal forces. As Chapter 3 covers, there are many good reasons to broaden one's experience and dip into many different fields. This type of experience enables workers to think creatively about problems and bring diverse perspectives into organizations. Unfortunately, it often means that companies won't worry too much about rewarding experts for the work they do by informally training other people. After all, if employees are just going to leave in a few years, why reward someone who's training them?

There are, however, some big exceptions to this rule.

The (Electric) General

Many companies care not just about educating their employees, but turning them into leaders. A few organizations excel at this feat to the extent that when one of their employees is hired as an executive at another company, the stock price of the hiring firm goes up by double-digit percentage points.

As of 2008, one out of every 27 CEOs of publicly traded companies had at some point worked in one of two companies: General Electric and IBM.[2] General Electric (GE) can count CEOs of Fortune 500 powerhouses such as Boeing, Pfizer, and Home Depot among its alumni. The basis for this success can be found in GE's dedication to nurturing its employees.

When GE identifies someone as a high-potential employee, they start rotating them through jobs in unrelated fields to build up their overall knowledge of the company. Current GE CEO Jeffrey Immelt, for example, started in the appliances division, moved to plastics, and finally ended up in medical systems. Even though training and integrating a new employee in these divisions takes time, GE strongly believes that this rotation is a key driver of their success.

Beyond changing team assignments, GE invests heavily in developing curricula and courses for its 150,000 employees. GE spends about $1 billion (with a "b") annually on corporate learning initiatives, which involves about 9,000 people a year physically traveling to GE "schools" for training, while about 60,000 people a year go through formal channels to enhance their skills.

As an organization, GE puts its money where its mouth is in regards to learning. It has numerous formal training programs that connect employees with the experts they need to succeed in their careers.

Interestingly, in mid-2012 this philosophy began to shift.[3] As expertise becomes more and more important, GE realized that competing at the highest levels with employees who had very little experience in a single business unit wasn't possible. Although top leaders must still be exposed to different business areas, the expectations are definitely lower than they were just a few years ago.

Although GE by any measure has been wildly successful over the last few decades, the need to constantly innovate at increasingly faster intervals has led executives to strongly focus on expertise. By keeping people in a particular division for longer periods of time, employees are encouraged to develop practical work experience and deep connections that will lead to even greater learning.

The problem for GE as well as other companies is that expertise development is typically attacked at a formal level. Training programs work great, but the company must be able to identify and keep experts long enough to make the training pay off. For practical experience to matter, a company must make sure that domain experts are actually teaching their less-experienced counterparts. The following sections investigate not only how these exchanges can be measured via the Sociometric Badges mentioned in Chapter 1, but also how you can reward employees for them.

The IT Firm Study

Try to imagine a company where interaction between employees didn't matter. It would probably be a company

- Where many people worked on individual tasks that didn't require them to talk to each other
- Where most of the work people did was on computers and with people in other places
- A lot like the one where my team from MIT took the Sociometric Badges

The organization we studied sells multimillion dollar servers through a distributed group of salespeople spread across the country. These salespeople talk with clients to figure out what they need their servers to do and then submit these specifications to a computer system. This system automatically assigns this task to one of the organization's engineers in its Midwest office, who actually lays out the physical hardware and tries to anticipate other requirements for the system. When he's done with the configuration, the engineer sends it back to the salesperson for negotiation with the client.

An engineer is assigned these tasks on a first-come, first-served basis. After he finishes a task, he goes to the back of the virtual line and waits for his next turn. These tasks are all logged by the computer system, which knows exactly when he started working on a task, when he completed it, whether he made any errors, and even the difficulty level. These tasks take anywhere from five minutes to eight hours to complete, and although difficult tasks often take longer than easy tasks, that's not always the case. To give employees extra motivation, their bonuses are determined entirely by how many of these tasks they can complete each day. From the company's perspective, any time not spent working on a task is time wasted.

From this process one would assume that people don't talk to each other. Why would they? Every second spent talking to a co-worker is dollars ticking off an employee's bonus check. There was a realization at this company, however, that something was amiss. Even though this division had only existed for a few months, some employees with high formal skill levels were struggling while employees with less experience on paper were the highest performers.

The IT firm wanted to understand these dynamics better, because clearly skill and task data alone weren't able to predict performance. The social element was missing. That's when our team from MIT went in with the Sociometric Badge.

IT Firm Study Results

We collected badge data for four weeks, accumulating thousands of hours of data. Over these four weeks, the division completed more than 1,000 tasks, which enabled us to build a performance profile for each employee by looking at how long on average it took people to complete these tasks.

In particular, the study focused on two types of behavior: individual behavior and social behavior. Individual behavior includes things such as movement levels, how workers tend to speak to other people, and how much time they spend at their desk. Social behavior, on the other hand, looked at who they spoke with and how well connected they were within the overall social network. Again, from the company's perspective, individual behavior and skills should be all that mattered. Any time spent talking to other people was essentially time wasted.

Imagine the company's surprise, then, when the strongest predictor of performance turned out to be whom an employee talked to. Specifically, how cohesive an employee's social network was had a major impact on productivity. In this case, the more the people an employee talks to talk with each other, the more productive the employee was. Also, it wasn't a small effect. If an employee spent 10% more time talking with her core group of contacts, she made the company roughly an extra $100,000 a month.

Those general results in hand, the next step was to understand what was driving differences in performance on specific tasks. Data from the company listed exactly who was working on a task and when they were doing it. This let us zoom in on the period of time that people were working on tasks and investigate whom they were talking to and how their behavior correlated with their performance.

Just looking at these patterns was extremely revealing. Plotting a social network diagram to look at who was speaking to whom when they were working on tasks revealed a bright center to this network. All communication paths eventually led to one of four individuals. Even more interestingly, the more central the person an employee spoke with, the more quickly she ended up completing her task. In fact, interacting with one of the four most central employees could cut task completion time by 66%.

These employees all had similar educational backgrounds and different levels of prior experience. They all had the exact same job title. From a formal perspective, they shouldn't have had any more or less of an effect than anyone else, but the badge data had revealed the informal experts.

Expert Puzzle

The study had uncovered not only an extremely accurate way to uncover experts, but also a method to very accurately predict performance on even short tasks. Although people at higher levels in the company had no idea that this expertise sharing was going on, these behaviors were central to the performance of the division. Even though exactly what these people were talking about during their conversations is unknown, the task data my MIT team collected strongly implies that it was work related. Remember, talking about something unrelated to the task only hurts an employee's performance and paycheck. Money can be a very strong incentive to stay on task. Beyond that, the predictive power of the results observed in the study only reinforces these findings, because they had a direct impact on performance for specific tasks.

These experts were spending a large portion of their time talking to other people. Perhaps it's not a surprise, then, that an expert's individual performance was only middle of the road. They were simply spending an inordinate amount of their time helping their coworkers.

Although for the organization this isn't necessarily a bad thing, it causes two problems. From the experts' point of view, they don't feel appreciated. Their guidance is helping to raise the performance of the entire division, but while their coworkers get rewarded, experts see no impact on their salary. They don't even get any formal recognition of their contributions from the company. It would be one thing if they got promoted due to their efforts, but their job title remained the same as everyone else.

The problem from the company's side is that without knowing it, management could easily cripple the performance of the entire division. Looking at the performance numbers, upper managers could have easily reassigned one of these experts to another role, which would eliminate the performance boost he or she gave to coworkers. The company just didn't know that these people were serving a critical function. Similarly, these experts could finally say enough is enough and leave for another company where their work would be appreciated. Both possibilities would be catastrophic for this division.

Being an Expert Expert

For this company and other organizations, a crucial first step toward fostering and retaining experts is to recognize their contributions. This could be as simple as a meeting where the team gets together and people publicly identify who's been helping them on their tasks, but even a little recognition shows that the company and their coworkers care about these experts.

That's not to say that experts should be rewarded with monetary incentives. The difficulty is that without the badge data, knowing the exact effect an expert has on other people is extremely difficult. Although ideally companies could reward that impact directly, there are some other ways to encourage the general behavior.

One particular change we recommended for the IT firm was in their bonus structure. At the time of this study, this department's rewards were 100% individual. Even if everyone else in the division did poorly, it had no effect on an employee's salary or bonus. The beauty of these experts, however, is that they raise the overall performance level of the entire division. So it makes sense that their overall performance should be an integral part of any bonus or salary discussion.

Rather than make salary and bonus entirely dependent on an individual's performance, we suggested making a large component of the bonus dependent on group performance. This could take the form of an overall performance target for the division or simply a graduated bonus that increases along with overall performance. Although this system would help experts receive more compensation, it also invites free riding. After all, experts end up getting the same bonuses as non-experts. Someone could easily coast along, not help anyone else out, and still get rewarded for the efforts of others.

In organizations this situation is, to a certain extent, unavoidable. Even without a bonus, an employee can choose to go out of her way to help coworkers or take an individual approach and focus on her own work. The hope is that by formally recognizing the value of expert contributions, an employee's focus, group versus individual, will come into play when being considered for promotions or work assignment.

As this study demonstrates, informal instances of advice giving and coworker learning can have massive effects on performance. Unfortunately, most companies focus exclusively on promoting learning at a formal level. Companies such as GE invest millions of dollars in massive training facilities and course programs to help their employees develop. These programs are certainly valuable and end up building the base skill level of the workforce, but they are still just a base.

In the IT firm study, all the employees had the same base, but a variety of experiences nurtured the expertise of a few individuals. By promoting and valuing that expertise, companies can get a level of education in their workforce that is nearly impossible to obtain in the classroom. Problems in these domains are so intricate and complex that one person can't exhaustively cover them all, but employees probably know someone who can help solve them.

This insight offers an important view into how to grow experts in an organization. The results from the IT firm study show that the most valuable experts aren't just knowledgeable; they're able to share that knowledge with their coworkers. The highest performers in the IT firm were probably experts themselves, but because they didn't share their knowledge with anyone, they had a very small effect on the overall performance of the division.

Successful companies supplement their training programs and educational initiatives with efforts to encourage knowledge sharing. These programs cultivate base expertise levels and financially encourage employees to share knowledge. However, going a step beyond that and creating formal and informal frameworks would make it easy for people to discover experts. Many companies go the formal route, listing expertise on intranet profile pages or the like, but in nearly all companies these pages are completely ignored or forgotten. Also, an employee who can find an expert through these systems might not be comfortable contacting a stranger.

Publicly identifying and praising experts in meetings is a better tactic. Companies could identify who the highest individual performers are in different areas and encourage people to ask them questions, because if their individual performance is high, they likely have valuable information to share. More informally, during meetings people could discuss who they went to for advice over the past week and how it helped them in their work. You might hear a lot of the same names getting called out, but injecting new people into the mix can help expand the pool of experts.

This practice is a major cultural shift. In many organizations, an employee who publicly praises a coworker for helping him do the job might be seen as weak. In fact, this is actually a sign of great strength. An employee can only do so much work alone, but people who are adept at finding and popularizing experts, and sources of knowledge in general, are essential for the overall performance of a group. In many ways, these people are meta-experts: experts at finding experts.

These meta-experts have the wherewithal to continuously discover new information and the ability to disseminate it to others. Experts have similar skills, but they also can't be afraid to advertise their experience. Compared to discussing advice one has received, this might seem like grandstanding. After all, an expert is announcing how much she knows and telling coworkers that they should look to her example for help in their work. Organizations need to shed that impression and instead realize that people need to communicate their skills. That is what ultimately drives performance in companies. It doesn't mean advertising one's self in a way that demeans colleagues, but looking for appropriate ways to share knowledge.

When we're particularly adept at certain problems, we must realize our power to help out coworkers. The potential for a positive impact is simply too big to ignore. On the other hand, acknowledging experts while also actively working to discover other experts is important. These experts are the tendons that span hundreds or thousands of individuals, ensuring that employees can continue running together as a whole. A company without those tendons, no matter how much it has built up its muscle, won't even be able to limp along.

6

You Look Like the Creative Type
Da Vinci versus the Hackathon

After building expertise in an established field, the next step in personal and corporate development is creating new expertise in an undiscovered field: creativity. Creativity is the engine of the world economy. Every company is trying to come up with the next big thing, and the next big thing often doesn't look at all like the current big thing.

Take the fast-changing world of mobile apps. In the span of a few years, it went from having a few proprietary apps on feature phones put there by a wireless carrier to ecosystems with millions of apps developed by companies ranging from large multinational game developers to teenagers coding in their spare time. The top-selling app this week will not be the top-selling app in a month. It's hard to imagine that same kind of rapid innovation in slower moving sectors such as car manufacturing or even computer hardware, but this constant need for the next big thing is spreading across these industrial boundaries.

Different types of creativity exist, not necessarily in terms of artistic creativity versus engineering creativity, but along the lines of how *disruptive*, or revolutionary, the creation is. This axis goes from incremental improvements, such as a bigger screen on a smartphone, to major innovations, such as the invention of the airplane.

One might be tempted to say that disruptive innovation is better and more important than smaller improvements, but that's not always the case. When a company is trying to move into a new area or break out of an unprofitable business model, the key to doing it is disruptive innovation. Plugging along with a broken model leads to being left behind by rivals. This was clearly the case with Nokia, which continued to churn out feature phones with uninspired designs long after the iPhone had disrupted the market.

Companies such as Amazon are fantastic at reaping the benefits of radical innovation. Releasing the Kindle, for example, represented a sea change in Amazon's strategy. No longer content to only sell content online, Amazon took the big leap and created their own eBook reader with a seamless online storefront that made purchasing incredibly fast and simple. Today, Amazon effectively owns this market, worth billions of dollars.

The first Kindle, however, wasn't that great to use. Buttons were in odd places, the screen took a long time to refresh, and the device itself was quite awkward and bulky. As soon as Amazon released the Kindle, competitors such as Barnes and Noble were fresh on their heels making similar devices. They even improved on some of the Kindle's mistakes. Amazon had to continue innovating, but not in the same way. They had to constantly improve the Kindle to make using it a better experience. This is where continuous improvement and incremental creativity come into play. This type of innovation is responsible for the long-term success of a company or product, but requires a completely different mindset.

For disruptive innovation to happen, breaking out of one's normal social circle and removing common assumptions are crucial. Incremental innovation, however, requires tight connections across a team that is working together to solve a problem. To be successful, organizations have to figure out how to effectively mix the two.

This mix strongly depends on what industry a company is in. In industries with longer release cycles, incremental improvement is paramount. Take the aircraft industry. Releasing a new airplane model represents the culmination of tens of billions of dollars of investment. Boeing's latest plane, the Dreamliner, cost a staggering $32 billion to develop. Each plane they sell costs on the order of $200 million, meaning Boeing will have to deliver more than 150 planes to break even in terms of raw revenue, not factoring into account opportunity cost or what their actual profit margin is on each plane. As of mid-2012 they have built a total of 18 planes. If Boeing were simply to switch gears and develop another new plane, they would very quickly be out of business. Instead they need to work on improving the Dreamliner, implementing small changes to make it more attractive to customers.

The pharmaceutical industry is at the other end of the spectrum. Incremental innovation can help create drugs that are combinations of previously released drugs, but these typically have low profit potential and don't fundamentally alter the market. Instead, drug makers are looking for that next home run, that next drug that meets a huge requirement in the marketplace and is radically different from anything else out there.

This task is hard to accomplish. Even the best pharmaceutical researchers only come out with a new drug once every 10 years. The rest of the time the compounds they work on never see the light of day, either because these compounds don't have the expected effects or those effects don't hold up under clinical trials. This makes gauging performance difficult and promoting effective development practice even more difficult. However, after a drug is released, the company's work is essentially done. It has to manage production and distribution, but it can't make any improvements to the drug.

In most organizations, ensuring a balance between these different types of creativity is important. Organizations that can get this balance right are destined to succeed in the long term. Interestingly, one of the best examples of this comes from the world of entertainment.

Cartoon Wars[1]

When you think of one of the most radically creative groups in the world, you might not think of South Park Studios (SPS), the company behind one of the highest-rated shows on Comedy Central. *South Park* is an animated show about a group of foul-mouthed fourth graders from the fictional Colorado town of the same name. The show has won a loyal following of millions of viewers, and critically it has garnered numerous awards, including four Emmys, a Peabody award, and an Oscar nomination for the feature film. *South Park* is probably best known for its crude art, liberal use of profanity, and explicit situations, as well as its merciless lampooning of pop culture icons.

The show is the brainchild of friends Trey Parker and Matt Stone. They made the original inspiration for the show, *The Spirit of Christmas*, out of construction paper and placed each individual frame by hand. Today their team of 70 uses off-the-shelf computers and digital editing tools to make *South Park* come to life—but Matt and Trey have retained their close engagement with the actual production of the show.

Production of an episode of *South Park* is unlike anything else in animated entertainment. An entire show is conceived, written, animated, recorded, and delivered to the broadcaster in six days. By comparison, an episode of *The Simpsons* is produced over the course of six *months*.

Creating an animated TV show is a complex process. In general, first someone must come up with a storyline and write a script. That script is then taken off to the storyboard department, which mocks up scenes with quick drawings. Working closely with the director, storyboard rapidly iterates on new scene conceptions to ensure that the visual presentation matches with the overall vision. Voicing work typically occurs simultaneously, which feeds into the animation process. After storyboards are complete, animators can work on drawing the different scenes that make up the show, but they need the audio track from the voice actors so that they can draw the characters' mouths appropriately. Although production staff members try to keep scripts and scenes relatively constant after the script has been finalized and storyboards are approved, last-minute changes invariably happen. Scripts and scene edits can change in the last few weeks before production whether from a demand from a censor or simply a change of heart from the director. These changes mean that the staff often won't see an episode until the final cut is ready to be sent to the broadcaster to air. In South Park Studios this entire process is turned on its head.

At SPS, as with all television shows, everything starts with writing. This part of the process relies heavily on disruptive thinking. Each episode has to be original. The more novel it is, the more it breaks away from other shows out there and touches a cultural nerve, the more likely it is to succeed.

The SPS writing staff of seven sits together in a meeting room on Thursday morning, trying to get the seed of an idea for next week's show. The first part of the discussion starts out with people just throwing out ideas they think are interesting even if they wouldn't be relevant to the show. In these discussions there aren't stupid or bad ideas, just unfunny ones. If an idea makes everyone laugh, then the team will keep pushing on that idea. By gauging the reaction of the team, they're able to figure out whether this idea is disruptive enough to be worth pursuing. The team comes to this decision mostly by paying attention to verbal and visual cues, not direct content. When the room gets energetic, that's when they know they have something.

Even though they have this egalitarian writing process, this team sometimes gets stuck. After creating hundreds of shows with very different storylines, coming up with wildly new ideas becomes increasingly difficult. That's when some of the writers will get up and start pacing around, trying to shake out of the funk through physical movement.

After the show concept is set, incremental creativity kicks in. There's not really any room for radically changing the direction of the episode, but there are slight refinements, both in terms of the dialogue in individual scenes to the look of the characters, that need to be iterated to create a polished final product.

At this point, script writing can start. While the writers are at work, however, the rest of the studio is also gearing up. Because episodes have to get completed in six days, there isn't time to separate the different aspects of production. Writing, animation, and voicing all have to be done as quickly as possible to make the Wednesday afternoon deadline, and that means constant overlap. To deal with that overlap, animators at SPS do everything.

Normally in animated shows, there are separate departments for storyboard, character design, and movie animation. Not so at SPS. Every animator has to be able to do all of these jobs and do them quickly. As the director of animation Jack Shih says: "If it takes you four days to get something done, you can't really contribute." Animators are brought in soon after the scriptwriting starts. After a rough story idea is fleshed out, animators have to go to work on storyboards. These storyboards are fed back to the writers, who use them to go over the story and make any changes they feel are necessary. At the same time, animators are already working on creating new characters for the show and drawing up the different scenes. Of course, animators rarely work with pen and paper anymore, and animators at SPS are no exception. By relying on computer models, animators are able to rapidly make changes to different scenes without having to repeat work. The art director works with the individual animators to iterate on fine points of scene composition, after which the finished scene is assembled into the overall episode video track. This demonstrates incredible incremental creativity, as the animation team works within its constraints to continuously refine their deliverables.

During this time, the cast of *South Park* is busy recording dialogue. Interestingly, in this case the cast and the writers are one and the same, with Matt and Trey providing the majority of the voices. Because they've been working together for more than 16 years, they're able to quickly communicate minute changes in the voice acting to make the dialogue more convincing. While they're writing, they can also immediately pitch dialogue and act it out, testing to see whether it comes out funny. Again, this is a powerful example of making extremely creative incremental changes.

Trey Parker is the captain of this ship. If he doesn't like something, it gets reworked by the whole team. Leads from the different departments sit together on a couch watching early cuts and quickly make determinations about what changes need to be made. This leads to a time crunch in the last few days of episode production. People often spend 24 hours a day eating, sleeping, and working at their desk. Although this schedule creates an extremely stressful environment for the 14 weeks a year the show is in production, it also creates a strong sense of camaraderie.

It also makes both disruptive and incremental innovation that much easier. People have the comfort level with their coworkers that they're not worried about throwing around "stupid" ideas, but they're also able to get on the same page when they need to execute.

The results of this process speak for themselves—a show that's still fresh after 16 years on the air, four Emmys, and a workforce that's incredibly engaged.

Compare *South Park* to a show like *The Simpsons*, which has been running for an incredible 23 years. *The Simpsons*, produced by Gracie Films, is a traditionally structured animated show with separate departments for the different art functions. After an initial story brainstorming session, each episode is assigned to an individual writer. In 1990 when the show was just starting up, there was still a core creative team that was able to span the gap between different departments.

Today, it's a different story. After a storyboard is completed and approved by directors, it is transferred to a Korean animation studio that does the actual animation that appears on your television. Although the level of involvement by the directors and animators at Gracie is unclear, they're certainly not under the same roof, as they are in SPS, and executing rapid, incremental innovation would be difficult if not impossible.

These process differences have a clear impact on the success of these shows. When comparing the Nielsen ratings of *The Simpsons* and *South Park*,[2] one must take a couple of things into account:

- Although the number of viewers watching *The Simpsons* has declined almost every year since its debut in 1989, this isn't just due to show quality. In 1989, the penetration rate of cable was very low, so grabbing a larger share of the market was much easier. That competition has increased over time.

- Before 2001, Nielsen-released ratings were based on the number of households that watched a show. Today, Nielsen releases the more accurate number of how many people actually watched.

To make these numbers roughly comparable, I multiplied the number of households by two to get a decent idea of how many people were watching *The Simpsons* (see Figure 6.1). This makes ratings from *The Simpsons* and *South Park* directly comparable.

What's fascinating when looking at these numbers is how consistent *South Park* has been relative to *The Simpsons*. *South Park* has managed to retain viewers over the course of its 16-year run with little change in its ratings over the past 10 years. *The Simpsons*, on the other hand, exhibits a fairly consistent downward trend in its ratings, with an audience in 2011 (season 23) that is only a quarter of what it was when the show premiered in 1989. Considering that the viewing population grew by about 26% during this same period of time, this represents an even more precipitous drop.

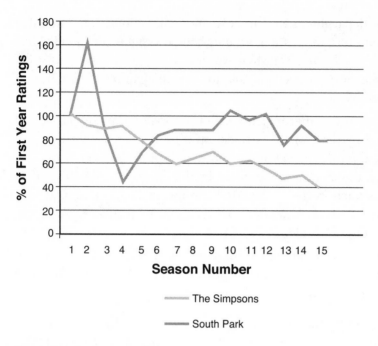

Figure 6.1 Simpsons Did It?

All of this is to say that when it comes to creativity, *South Park* wins the cartoon wars.

Lessons from South Park: The Roots of Creativity

The case of SPS is compelling, but it is a one-off success. Pretty much every company in the world needs its employees to innovate, to be creative, be it in a more disruptive fashion or one that's more incremental. Creativity isn't included in school curricula or college requirements, however. Even intelligence tests gauge people's ability to process information and remember rules, not to innovate and think up new ideas.

This bias against creativity instruction bleeds over into the way organizations think about training. Training sessions are much more about specific facts or systems that employees need to know, not how to think. Although organizations know that creativity is important, they just don't have a solid model of what creativity actually looks like. Without that model, creating sustainable improvements in creativity is extremely difficult for organizations.

That's not to say that companies can't take lessons from SPS. Their model of rapid incremental innovation, breaking down organizational silos for disruptive show ideas, and close connections between coworkers sets it apart from other shows. This certainly seems like the secret sauce that makes the studio so successful.

As already mentioned, however, different organizations need different types of innovation, different types of creativity. Although inferring general rules from these examples is possible, getting into the data to see what is really making everything tick is necessary.

To tackle this problem, my collaborators at Arizona State (ASU) used the badges to look at researchers in different research and development (R&D) labs across the U.S.[3] Their question, similar to the one posed in this chapter, was around what behaviors were actually driving creativity. After the relevant behaviors are known, they can be incorporated into training, management policies, and even the educational system.

Researching R&D

R&D is the lifeblood of the modern company, not to mention a hotbed of creative activity. With few exceptions, major companies today devote a large fraction of their budget to an internal R&D division. Normally these labs are tasked both with creating improvements to existing products (the "D") and coming up with completely new ideas that might or might not ever make it into production (the "R").

Measuring return on investment for R&D is difficult, mostly because an investment made today might not pay off until 10 years from now, whereas other efforts can show up in a product in 6 months. So, sales numbers don't really give a company much to evaluate. Even if they did, in the 10 years a company spends working to make an innovation become reality, it can't use data from that project to improve the creativity of the workforce.

This problem is magnified at the individual level. When an individual researcher comes up with a new invention, it often has to be used in tandem with other technologies to be useful. How do you determine how big of a contribution that invention was?

As you can imagine, with such a big gap between measurement and reality, researchers have developed a number of tools to gauge creativity. Essentially these tools are all subjective, but by using a number of tools to triangulate measurements and testing across a variety of contexts, one can feel more confident in the results. Specifically, researchers use self-reports on creativity and have experts code daily logs of activity to assess how creative someone was on a given day. Survey questions essentially take the form of "How creative were you today?" Activity logs, on the other hand, ask employees to write details about what they did during the day. These methods are really only applicable for research projects because these surveys and activity logs take a substantial amount of time to fill out.

Using the Sociometric Badges and the aforementioned evaluation tools, ASU researchers Win Burleson and Pia Tripathi studied three R&D teams in different technology organizations. The goal was to understand creativity in general and see whether the data collected with the badges could actually predict this nebulous concept.

The teams they studied had between five and seven members and were broadly focused on technology R&D. One team worked on software creation, while the two other teams were concerned with thinking up new systems that included both hardware and software. The workplaces for these teams were similar as well. Each team member had his or her own cubicle facing a wall, with the cubicles surrounding a central collaboration space. The idea behind this setup was to create an environment that facilitates close collaboration but also provides for individual space to focus on different work efforts.

The ASU team had a couple of hypotheses going into this study:

- During highly creative days, team members would interact more closely with one another. That is, the average amount of time people spent speaking with their coworkers would increase.

- On these highly creative days, people would also be much more physically active.

These hypotheses intuitively make a lot of sense and match the observations from SPS. When people are having a creative day, they're working very closely with colleagues and rapidly iterating on new ideas. The better the ideas, the more enthusiastic people become, which in real terms means speech and movement are much more energetic.

The ASU team set out to put some numbers behind these observations, finally injecting hard data into what has long been considered a "soft" metric.

Gauging Creativity: The Results

After the ASU researchers analyzed the data, they were able to not only confirm their hypotheses, but demonstrate that behavioral data from the badges was extremely predictive of creative output. Specifically, the amount of time spent interacting with team members and expending movement energy was strongly positively correlated with creativity. When the researchers used this data to build an algorithm to recognize creative days, they were able to obtain greater than 90% accuracy.

This result is a major step forward because it means that your creativity can be measured just by looking at whom you talk to and how much you move around. While things besides creativity can obviously affect a person's movement patterns, these results indicate that those other factors don't have a consistent effect.

Some people don't even realize that they're being creative, as illustrated by the disparities between the expert and self-report data. This implies that behavioral data analysis may be a much more accurate and less time-intensive approach for measuring creativity.

This method would also be extremely helpful for understanding creative events. By automatically detecting when people are creative, companies could better study the conditions that gave rise to that creativity. On a large scale, with organizations composed of hundreds of thousands of people, this action could yield creative iteration on many different processes to help spur creativity across the company.

This data also provides some tools to help people figure out how to get out of a creative funk. For example, rather than trying to work through new ideas on your own, engaging other people in discussion is best. This could be as simple as going to a meeting room and working on a whiteboard. Even scheduled brainstorming sessions can help.

Longer term creative success also depends upon people in different groups interacting with each other. If you only interact with people in your social circle, you end up speaking to people who all have the same opinion. The lack of these interactions is precisely what causes companies such as Nokia to ignore a major disruptive force in their market. As discussed earlier, although Nokia had dominated the cell phone market for some time, the strength of its organizational silos meant that until recently their dominance wasn't turned into a transformative opportunity to make smartphones central to the company's strategy.

Serendipitous interactions are incredibly important for making random connections that pay off down the road. You could meet someone working in a completely different area and find out that you're working on things that are actually quite related or could solve one another's problems. Longer-term studies are needed to determine the impact on the company's bottom line, but preliminary data shows that people who tend to have these random interactions perform better than people who don't (see Chapter 4).

Although interaction patterns and physical movement were both predictive of creativity, they need to be addressed separately. It's not surprising that you're more creative when you're more energetic and moving around. After all, when you're lying around on a couch and not lifting a finger, you're probably not being very productive or creative. An example of the importance of energy comes from the crucible of startup innovation, the hackathon. One of the hallmarks of creative software companies is the liberal use of caffeine-fueled 24-hour programming jams called *hackathons*. These events, at companies such as Facebook and Google, get a bunch of engineers together in a large room with plenty of computers, couches, pizza, and drinks, and encourage people to collaborate in small teams and build a working demo of the next big thing.

During a 24-hour period, programmers devise code and demonstrate a working application that builds on top of a company's infrastructure. This Herculean undertaking yields important innovations—Facebook's chat feature, for example—and at the same time builds social capital across the company. These are intense events, with people furiously coding to meet deadlines and quickly iterating on features to hack something workable and intuitive together. No wonder that the startup community has enthusiastically embraced hackathons as a major tool to promote innovation.

Hackathons are an example of the type of activity that is associated with higher energy levels and higher creativity. The results from the ASU study don't say that people should spend the entire day running around the office. Instead they're saying that rather than sitting still at your desk, you should try to walk around a bit more and get yourself amped up about the work you're doing. These tasks can be challenging, but that's another reason why events such as hackathons can be effective. They set a cultural expectation for high energy and high commitment, and this activity is infectious. When everyone around you is energetic, you similarly become more energetic.

In contrast to these findings, in many socities the lone genius is often seen as the ultimate model of creativity. Leonardo da Vinci, Edison, these are the giants of individual innovation. Forgotten is the fact that these people lived in an extremely vibrant and collaborative community. Da Vinci traveled around Italy during the heady days of the Renaissance, interacting and working with many of the brilliant luminaries of that time. Edison's work developed during the boom times of the Industrial Revolution, and he similarly was heavily embedded in the scientific and industrial communities. Edison's famous work on the light bulb was actually a practical improvement built on top of existing technology, not something that he invented from scratch.

As the data from the ASU study shows, innovation isn't just about the individual. That's not to say that individual people aren't important. People actually have to work to be creative and make innovations a reality. At its core, creativity is about getting the right people energized to collaborate and make something great. The combination of different skills and the chaotic mixing of ideas is what generates innovations that change the world.

7

Tough It Out versus Stay at Home

Modeling Disease Spread Through Face-to-Face Conversations

When you get sick, do you go to work?

Although on its face this is a simple question, it has a far from simple answer. What humans are instinctually driven to do isn't necessarily a product of an evolutionary response to disease, nor is it based solely on our upbringing. The culture of our company and country can play a huge role.

From a physical health perspective, obviously staying home is better. There are no debates. If you stay at home when you're sick, you are unable to infect anyone else. Many public health professionals would argue that by staying home you're making a positive decision for society. Fewer people get sick, fewer people miss work, and all it costs you is one day of productivity.

However, the actual cost might be far higher. From a productivity perspective, whether you go to work has a huge impact not just on yourself, but on your coworkers. As discussed in Chapter 4, when you don't interact with people that you work with, everyone's performance suffers. A lack of communication also negatively impacts job satisfaction levels, and consequently, mental health outcomes.

Companies continually grapple with this quandary, as the following personal experience illustrates. A few years ago I took time off from my graduate studies at MIT to work as a researcher for a large Japanese electronics company in a lab near Tokyo. I had collaborated with some researchers from this lab, and in order for us to work together at a more meaningful level, I had to be an employee. As an undergraduate, I had minored in Japanese, so I was also thrilled at the opportunity to return to Japan and shore up my language skills. I had worked in other labs in Japan before, and because I could speak the language, I felt like I was prepared for the cultural differences that awaited me there.

Japanese offices, and Japanese research labs in particular, are very different from those we have in the U.S. A typical lab has an extremely large bullpen area, with hundreds or even thousands of researchers sitting across straight rows of open desks. Desks might have a small cubicle wall, but if you stand up, you can easily see everyone in the lab.

Face time is also highly valued. Researchers arrive fairly early, around 8 a.m., but normally won't leave until around 8 p.m. Everyone eats lunch and dinner together in the cafeterias. The environment is designed to foster interaction and keep people at work for as long as possible.

One day during my time at this Japanese research lab, I got sick. Not the kind of sick where you have a light headache that you can quickly kill off with some aspirin, but the 101-degree fever sit in your bed wearing an oversize sweatshirt while watching *Law and Order* reruns kind of sick. My conundrum was that my team had a presentation coming up the next day, so I had to finish up the materials we needed to show our manager.

After seeing that I was looking pale and generally out of sorts, one of my colleagues came over to my desk to see what was the matter.

"I'm coming down with something," I told him honestly. "I've got to stay here and finish the slide deck, but I probably won't be able to make the presentation tomorrow." He looked at me very seriously.

"No, you have to go home right now," he replied. I was a bit confused, and I thought that maybe I had made a mistake in my Japanese. You weren't allowed to bring company computers home with you or e-mail attachments outside the company, so finishing up at home was out of the question.

"I really need to finish this by tomorrow, so I have to stay and finish it today," I reiterated. He shook his head.

"No, you really have to go home right now," and with that I was politely excused from the lab. In a mild state of shock, I took the train back to my apartment and considered how I should respond. I knew that I had to finish this presentation, so I figured the best course of action would be to arrive at the lab early the next day and leave myself enough time to complete everything.

When I arrived, I was politely told that I had to wait at least one day before coming back. They just wouldn't let me back into the lab under any circumstances until they were convinced I was healthy. In Japanese companies, the desire for face time and even productivity is vastly outweighed by a mysophobia (fear of germs) that borders on the extreme.

For those of us from the U.S, this hard-line reaction to illness seems strange. Imagine telling your boss: "Hey, I know we've got an important deadline tomorrow, but I'm feeling under the weather, so I won't be able to make it." You would at least expect a bemused reproach, if not a downright reprimand.

United States workers doggedly insist on meeting professional obligations even if they have personal issues that could conflict with these obligations. When a child is born, parents aren't guaranteed pay for the time they take off, and after 12 weeks, their employer could legally fire them if they haven't returned to work. So it's no surprise that when we come down with an illness, employers are less than forgiving.

In a different personal example, I was on a business trip where I had to work while running a fever of 102 degrees for three days. Somehow I managed to be halfway productive, but for the week after I returned home, I was in a constantly weakened state, not to mention the fact that I probably infected a number of my colleagues. This would cause a ripple effect in terms of lost productivity. Instead of only one person out of commission for a few days, all of a sudden you have a dozen people working at vastly reduced effectiveness and feeling miserable in general.

It's easy to understand why companies cultivate a "tough it out" ethos. Unless you can work from home, your productivity when you're out sick is zero. As shown in all the studies mentioned in this book, even working from home isn't very effective because face-to-face communication with your coworkers dramatically improves your performance as well as that of all the people with whom you normally interact. If you stay at work, even though your effectiveness will be reduced, you can still take advantage of all the social productivity effects that the studies in this book uncovered.

So, which response is correct?

To answer that question, real-world behavioral data is needed to understand how diseases spread within companies, using methodologies developed by epidemiologists. This allows us to estimate how changes in behavior from disease responses impact productivity. Using data from the IT firm introduced in Chapter 5, that's exactly what we did.

Corporate Epidemiology[1]

The IT firm project is a great dataset for investigating the effectiveness of disease response strategies. Recall that in this study dozens of people configuring complex hardware systems wore Sociometric Badges for about a month. Besides the badge data, we also had hard productivity numbers, allowing us to create a very accurate model of performance based on behavior.

When people get sick, their behavior changes. To see what sort of effect this would have, we can modify the behavioral patterns extracted from the original IT firm data and observe how productivity would change. Specifically, we look at how the cohesion changes for each member of the firm, because that was the feature most strongly correlated with performance.

In this exercise we simulate people getting sick in the original dataset, simulate the infection spreading, and calculate the effect this illness has on performance. The goal is to see what happens if people change their behavior when an outbreak occurs. For example, if people go straight home when they become sick, we can remove their interactions from the original dataset for the days when they are "at home." This changes the interaction patterns in the entire group, and using our performance model, we can see how this behavior change affects the bottom line.

To simulate the spread of the disease, fellow MIT researchers Manuel Cebrian, Riley Crane, and I collaborated with epidemiologists Leon Danon and Ellen Pollock from Harvard's School of Public Health. One major aspect of this model was determining how to simulate disease transmission and recovery. Luckily, the public health field has studied these processes extensively. Transmission probabilities are derived from transmission methods and virus lifecycle estimates in the academic literature (the now-famous R_0 value popularized in the movie *Contagion*). Recovery times are also relatively easy to estimate. Researchers will observe infected individuals in controlled environments, typically a laboratory, and take blood samples over the course of a few days to see how long someone takes to recover.

We used a standard infectious disease simulation method called an SIR (Susceptible-Infected-Recovery) model. Each stage of the SIR model has different properties, and at any point in time any individual is in the S, I, or R stage. In the S stage you're not sick, but you might become infected (although for certain types of disease, not everyone is susceptible). After you're infected, you enter the I stage. At this point you can infect other people for a set period of time. Each time you interact with a person in the S stage, the simulation program picks a random number to determine whether that person becomes infected. In reality even after you contract the disease, you are not immediately infectious because the disease needs time to spread through your body. However, this doesn't make a big difference in the outcome of any simulation because for most illnesses becoming infectious takes only an hour or two.

After a few days, you enter the Recover stage. In this stage you can't infect other people or be infected, and this is the virtual analogue of the immunity you acquire after having been exposed to an illness. Many of us have experienced this in our own lives. After you have a fever, it's not uncommon that one of your family members will get sick as well. Even though other family members might catch the bug too, you stay healthy because your immune system has learned to fight off the disease.

In terms of hard numbers, interacting with an infected individual for one minute in our model gives you a 0.7% chance of infection. Full recovery after infection, on the other hand, takes three days.

These numbers are roughly equivalent to the epidemiological characteristics of H1N1.

Now that we have the data and the model, how do we start things off? In other words, how do we choose who gets sick first so that we can see how the disease will spread? The answer is that we don't. For every individual in the data, in the beginning of every day for a one-week period, we start a simulation with that person labeled "infected." This creates different paths of infection through the workplace, because we don't really know who is more likely to get sick beforehand. Each of these infection starting points is simulated a few hundred times. The reasoning behind this method is that depending on how lucky you are, different people will get randomly infected when simulating this epidemic. Even with real data, there is a chance that many more people will get randomly infected in a single simulation simply because the random number generator happened to pull the right numbers out of a hat. We need to average over these different simulations to ensure an accurate picture emerges of what we would expect to happen. Adding in the extra wrinkle that different people are the starting points for infections provides a robust view into the dynamics of this disease.

During the initial simulations, we didn't change behavior at all. We just wanted to see what the dynamics of the disease propagation looked like: Were certain individuals responsible for most of the disease spreading? Did certain types of interactions lead to the majority of infections?

What we observed was initially very puzzling. Although longer interactions did tend to lead to infections, the shorter interactions were responsible for the lion's share of disease propagation. It makes sense that longer interactions would lead to infections. Mathematically, if an infected person talks to a healthy individual for more than 100 minutes, then a greater than 50% chance exists that the healthy person will become infected. Compare this probability to what happens if I talk to 20 people for 5 minutes each: The likelihood that I will infect a single person is the same—50%. The likelihood that I would infect a specific individual, on the other hand, is only 3.5%. However, if I infect one of the first people I talk to, then after our

5-minute conversation, we can both go on and infect other people. These dynamics are what caused most of the infections we observed.

As we were wrapping our heads around this concept, we wondered what would happen if we were able to reduce those interactions. Rather than completely cutting off all interaction as we initially proposed, we wanted to investigate the effect of removing only these very short conversations. We didn't have a good idea of exactly what the cutoff should be, so we simply tried them all.

Figure 7.1 shows the number of people who got sick (the epidemic final size—vertical axis) as we put a higher and higher threshold on the minimum duration of a conversation (horizontal axis). So for the point of minimum contact duration of 5 minutes, we eliminated all interactions that lasted less than 5 minutes and repeated the simulation. As you can see, this 5-minute period seemed to be the perfect cutoff point, reducing the number of people who got sick by almost 50%. After this 5-minute period, only slight reductions occur in the epidemic's size.

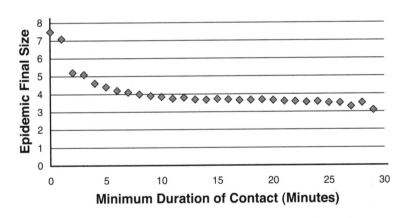

Figure 7.1 Reducing disease spread by removing short interactions

We also wanted to see what happened if we put a maximum threshold on interactions, eliminating only conversations that were longer than a certain amount of time. As you can see from Figure 7.2, we don't observe a similar effect. To achieve a result equivalent to what we observed at 5 minutes in the graph shown in Figure 7.1, every interaction longer than 25 minutes would have to be eliminated.

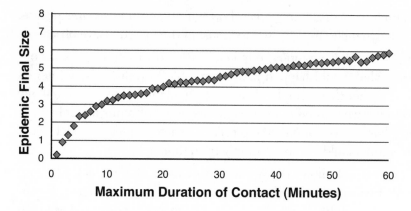

Figure 7.2 Reducing disease spread by removing long interactions

Still, the question about the effect on productivity remains. What would this kind of behavior change (that is, removing conversations of a certain duration) do to the productivity of the division? In these same simulations we also computed how the networks of the division changed. By speaking a little bit less, or not at all, to other people in the division, performance was substantively affected.

Figure 7.3 shows the percentage change in the division's overall performance that results from removing interactions falling below a duration threshold. The minimum duration of conversation numbers show a very interesting bump in productivity around the five-minute mark. According to the data, productivity would actually *improve* by eliminating these very short interactions.

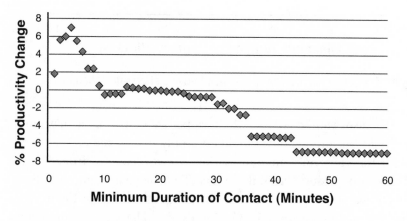

Figure 7.3 Removing short interactions improves productivity?

Here is the disconnect between modeling and reality: Shorter interactions tend to be largely informal, such as bumping into someone you know in the hallway or chatting by the coffee machine. For people whom we are very close to, we'll have deeper conversations in addition to these short ones. People with whom we only casually chat, however, probably don't run in the same social circles, which is why removing those interactions would yield an increase in cohesion. This would imply that we should universally strive to eliminate these short conversations.

In the short term, there are certainly advantages to this practice. People would be able to spend more time talking to their close contacts, making it easier to communicate complex information and building trust. On the other hand, eliminating these interactions would slowly erode the connectivity of the overall division. After these weak connections are removed, the group would eventually become an echo chamber because group members would only be talking to each other. As we've already discussed, that would be a huge mistake.

Therefore, we should interpret these results more in the context of epidemic risk than as a general rule for how to shape communication patterns. The results clearly state that during high-risk periods, reducing the number of short interactions will greatly decrease the number of people who get sick and might even have some performance benefits. At the very least we wouldn't expect productivity to suffer.

Eliminating longer interactions, however, is a different story. As Figure 7.4 shows, eliminating longer interactions has a consistently negative effect. This effect comes from the fact that you can spend long periods of time talking with the people with whom you work closely, and a reduction in those interactions will almost always decrease the cohesiveness of your network. For comparison, removing interactions longer than 30 minutes would result in a 1% decrease in productivity.

Now that we know what effect these different interventions have on health and productivity, the question becomes how to implement them. The focus shouldn't just be on reducing the number of short conversations. Although this represented a nice tradeoff between health and performance, in some circumstances health concerns will preempt performance issues. In those cases reducing *both* shorter interactions and longer ones would be helpful in an effort to clamp down on the spread of a disease. This is when staying at home becomes an attractive option.

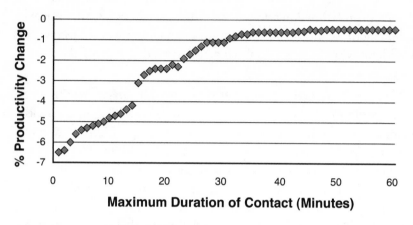

Figure 7.4 The negative effect of removing long interactions

Many strategies are available for reducing the number of short conversations. As previously discussed in Chapter 4, distance has a powerful influence on interactions. The closer you sit to someone, the more likely you are to speak with that person. This is especially true for short interactions. If you're going to spend an hour in a meeting with someone, the distance to his desk doesn't matter. Walking over to him or finding a meeting room is worth your while. However, distance has a huge impact on serendipitous interactions. When your desk is physically closer to people you know, you're more likely to bump into them or engage in some chitchat.

We can use this tendency to our advantage by piggybacking on current trends in the workplace, namely the concept of open seating. In open seating offices, no one has an assigned desk. Instead, different groups sit in different areas, and people in a particular group can choose any desk in their area either for a single day or for at most a few weeks. Instead of keeping groups together, mixing up the different groups would increase the average distance between people on the same team. This would mean fewer serendipitous interactions because you would be farther away from the people you normally talk to.

This seating arrangement wouldn't be the policy all the time, and would only apply during high-risk periods. At the beginning of an outbreak, companies could shift their work areas to "epidemic seating." This costs the companies practically nothing, doesn't inconvenience employees, and has a positive impact on health. You could also imagine some side benefits from this effort, because you might get to know people in other groups whom you don't normally talk to. We might think this would defeat the purpose of the new seating arrangement, but these would actually tend to be longer interactions because you have to introduce yourself at length. In any case short interactions will occur more infrequently than they would in a normal seating arrangement.

Another simple strategy for reducing short conversations involves keeping office doors closed. An open door makes it easy for people to poke their head in and say hello, which under normal circumstances would be welcome. By keeping office doors closed, someone can still easily come by, but it would be a more intentional interaction, which would typically last for a longer period of time.

To make a major reduction in the number of short conversations, another effective strategy is to increase the number of long interactions. During high-risk periods, companies could schedule "Meeting Days" where every meeting for the next few weeks is crammed into a few days. This approach would create a large number of very long interactions, but would all but eliminate short conversations. If for various logistical reasons this is not possible to fully implement, even a partial shift of meetings to high-risk periods would have a marked effect.

Making small changes to reduce long interactions, on the other hand, is relatively hard. These interactions tend to be planned and more critical than short ones. Therefore, you have to change intention and formal processes more than changing the environment slightly to encourage certain behaviors. A simple step would be to eliminate meetings longer than a certain amount of time. You could also move meetings to video conference, but that would significantly degrade the quality of the meeting.

Given the impact on performance, however, reducing long interactions represents a fairly drastic step and would only be taken in extreme cases. In general, this means that the best way to eliminate long interactions is for people to stay at home. However, impacting the primary mechanism of airborne infections is also possible through cultural changes.

In Japan people wear surgical masks when they're sick so that they pass fewer germs to others. Because the mask blunts the velocity of expelled air and most infections are caused from talking to other people, this intervention would actually be quite effective.

Table 7.1 summarizes different strategies that organizations can adopt to combat disease while balancing the impact on productivity. Depending on the situation, a company might want to place more emphasis on health, but in another situation context may become more important. The strategies presented here shouldn't be viewed as a list of things that have to be implemented for every disease outbreak, but rather part of a toolbox that organizations can adapt to their specific needs.

Table 7.1 What to Do in an Epidemic

Type of Interaction Priority	Encouraging Productivity	Protecting Health
Reduce Short Interactions	Make seating changes, close office doors, schedule "Meeting Days"	Make seating changes, close office doors
Reduce Long Interactions	—	Cancel/reschedule meetings, have video conference meetings, send sick employees home
Cultural Changes	Wear surgical masks	Wear surgical masks

Cultural changes such as wearing face masks are imperative for preventing the next pandemic from simultaneously crippling our health and economy. These cultural changes don't just need to feel good, they need to be based on hard data. Simulations help support these changes, but real data from actual epidemics is also needed to improve our responses. This chapter lists some effective strategies that take a unique approach to combating illness—and covering your mouth when you cough is also never a bad idea.

8

Why We Waste $1,200,000,000,000 a Year

Mergers and Acquisitions, Corporate Culture, and Communication

Companies don't grow to a massive size all by themselves. Nearly every company in the world with more than 10,000 employees (and many that are smaller than that) have either merged with or acquired another company, or many. This activity, called mergers and acquisitions (M&A for short), is one of the most important and difficult processes in business.

Every year, about $2 *trillion* worth of M&A activity occurs. Some of this activity is truly epic in scale, with gargantuan deals such as AOL's acquisition of Time Warner for $164.7 billion in 2000 standing out not just for its monstrous size but also for its monumental failure. Failure in M&A is actually the rule rather than the exception, with most estimates pegging M&A failure north of 60%. In fact, the three largest mergers and acquisitions[1] of all time either ended in breakup or resulted in financial catastrophe, costing the companies involved a combined $466 billion.

These failures cost the world economy $1.2 trillion *every year*, enough money to pay for the college tuition of every student in the United States and still have a bit left over to solve Greece's debt crisis. Wasting that amount of money is criminal and demands a solution.

Of course, companies don't set out to blow billions of dollars on a questionable deal. They spend a great amount of time researching and negotiating with potential M&A partners. Some of this work is done by M&A experts, who charge millions of dollars to investigate the financial performance and potential synergies that could be realized through M&A. Many of these deals are years in the making, with a vast amount of careful planning and formal procedures put in place to make sure M&A goes smoothly.

Yet these plans fail repeatedly, and companies continue to follow the same doomed path as those before them. Business leaders mostly shrug and take the common refrain: "M&A is just hard." This statement is fair enough, because many things are just hard. Building a supersonic jet is hard. Designing a computer processor with hundreds of millions of parts is hard. The thing is, those things still get done well, with vastly higher success rates than occurs with M&A.

My perspective on this problem is a little different. Consider the state of M&A: Thousands of some of the smartest people in the world work on exactly the same problem and consistently fail. Either M&A is impossible and companies should just resign themselves to blowing $1.2 trillion a year, or they are focusing on the wrong things.

Let's start with one particularly famous example of M&A: eBay's acquisition of Skype.

I'll Call, and Raise

Skype is familiar to many of us as the ubiquitous voice-over-IP (VoIP) program used for free video chat and incredibly cheap phone calls to anywhere in the world. Skype was founded in 2003 by a small group of European programmers who quickly built the software into a communication juggernaut. Today it has become a wildly successful platform, with more than 13% of all international calls being made through Skype.

Back in 2005, however, a potential suitor in the form of eBay appeared on Skype's doorstep. This is the same eBay that makes the overwhelming majority of its money from an online marketplace where people buy and sell all variety of products, from toothbrushes to TVs to entire towns. What connection does online communication have to a community of buyers and sellers, you ask? According to then eBay CEO Meg Whitman, it would allow for people to make much higher value, complex deals through their online marketplace:

Buying a used bulldozer, for example, could take a high degree of involvement from both buyer and seller because it's expensive and complex. Doing this entirely through e-mail or IM could be difficult. Using Skype will be quicker and easier and very cost effective.[2]

Okay, so one must assume that bulldozer purchases are not going to be that common on eBay. Although eBay has had its share of off-the-wall transactions, even from a cursory glance, it seems like there's not going to be too much natural synergy between these two companies. Strangely, however, analysts were by and large very positive about this acquisition. JPMorgan analyst Imran Khan wrote:

We believe eBay will leverage Skype's products to improve both customer service and buyer/seller communication. Also, Skype has various products in its pipeline which we believe will add more efficiencies to eBay's platform (e.g., video, which could be used for product demos).

Will Stofega from the research firm IDC echoed this sentiment:

Beyond adding an application for eBay customers, Skype entails a new revenue stream for eBay and another way of getting beyond the portal. They wanted to get into the game to become a more full service portal.

These reactions left me scratching my head. Were we looking at the same acquisition? Integrating products, especially ones that are as different as VoIP and an online marketplace, is extremely difficult. Besides both having a bit of messaging functionality, Skype is a completely different beast.

On top of that, Skype has its headquarters is Luxembourg, whereas eBay is based in San Jose. Despite the fact that eBay was buying a company that specialized in improving communication across distance, Skype can't fix a time difference of nine hours. This means that exactly zero overlap in workday occurs between the two companies, even assuming people come in at 8 a.m. Any integration is going to take a lot of late night/early morning hours and a lot of travel. As discussed in Chapter 4, this is a recipe for a long, hard road ahead.

The analysts, however, were not looking at these obstacles. They were looking at the financials, at the long-term strategic implications of such a deal. As such, most of them didn't blink at eBay's offer of approximately $3.1 billion dollars to acquire Skype.

Let's fast forward a few years to the fall of 2009. The acquisition of Skype by eBay has not gone well. There are no major joint product offerings to speak of, and Skype's revenue has failed to expand at a pace rapid enough to offset the huge amount of cash that eBay laid down for the purchase. eBay cuts its losses and agrees to sell 70% of Skype to Silver Lake Partners, a private investment firm. eBay's loss on the sale: approximately $1.2 billion. For those of you keeping score, this acquisition is essentially equivalent to eBay putting $300 million in a paper shredder every year that it owned Skype.

Given the challenges identified earlier in this discussion, these difficulties shouldn't have come as a surprise. Beyond the time zone problem, eBay and Skype are very different companies. This might seem like a surprise to many, because they're both tech startups with employees that have relatively similar educational backgrounds. Beneath that, however, lie different norms around communication and information exchange.

As you might expect, employees at Skype like to use Skype—a lot. They assiduously update their status messages, save chat logs for later consumption, and generally thrive on quick long-distance communication. In addition, Skype the company focuses on remaining informal and decidedly free of jargon in its interactions. Rather than take pride in uber-geekiness, Skype takes pride in helping people communicate.[3]

eBay is very different. Compared to Skype's miniscule team of 150 programmers, eBay at the time had more than 10,000 employees working in sales, marketing, and of course, programming. Companies of this size often develop a more formal character, and eBay was no exception. In fact, eBay's executives went so far as to mock the "amateurish" board meetings at one of their startup partners, something that came to light after their bitter breakup with Craigslist.[4]

Although the lack of strategic synergies in actual technological offerings no doubt had a major hand in sinking eBay's acquisition of Skype, these cultural factors cannot be underestimated. In general, if a company doesn't communicate effectively, problems are bound to occur.

Ironically, Skype has recently been the subject of increased M&A activity from another tech giant: Microsoft. In 2011 Microsoft made a whopping $8.5 billion offer for Skype, which was subsequently accepted and universally panned by analysts (perhaps wanting to avoid the same error twice).

From a cultural perspective, however, some hope exists that a Microsoft–Skype marriage could succeed. For one thing, Microsoft is a truly global company, with major offices in Europe and all parts of the world. This would make communication and integration of a new Skype business unit much easier than that attempted by eBay six years earlier. Of course, the formal/informal dynamic at Microsoft is similar to eBay's, so time will tell whether this acquisition adds to the ever-growing tally of losses due to M&A.

Fixing the Problem

Apart from the financials and all the formal check boxes needed for M&A to be successful, companies can take a number of other steps to ensure a long-lasting relationship. Before even thinking about merging, understanding the cultures of the companies involved and how well they mesh is important. This is addressed in many of the preceding chapters in this book, so I won't rehash it all here. Suffice it to say that understanding whether the companies are socially similar, whether people communicate in similar ways, and how people collaborate is critical. Differences in one of these areas will require special attention, and if the separation is too wide, companies should seriously question the long-term prospects of this deal.

Suppose your company decides to go ahead with the acquisition. Teams are put together, merging the actual organizations into a single unit. This usually means redesigning the org charts, opening new offices, and changing everything around so that formally these two organizations are now one. What needs to be investigated, however, is whether this integration has actually occurred on a collaborative level.

If the new, combined organization is still acting like two companies, then a problem exists. This was, in fact, the subject of a study done by my collaborator Sinan Aral from MIT.[5] Interestingly, this study was not about M&A at all. He and his co-authors were investigating how e-mail communication related to the productivity of individual workers. When they looked at the communication data as a network, they saw something extremely interesting. The organization looked as if it were split into two groups, with little communication passing between the different parts of the organization.

Curious, after the study was completed, they returned to the company to see how they were progressing. They were informed that things had not been going so well, and in fact the company had split up. Sinan already knew where they had split it: into the two groups that he had seen in the communication network data.

Clearly, attention must be paid to the social integration between merging companies. By observing how this changes over time, the M&A team can quickly intervene if it seems like the formerly separate organizations are not interacting effectively. If teams are separated over distance, then getting them together face to face after the merger can ensure that they're able to develop higher levels of trust, as discussed in Chapter 4. Even better, mixing desks between the two companies can increase the number of serendipitous interactions across former organizational boundaries.

What causes these integration dynamics to arise in the first place? Of course, the cultures of both organizations play into it, as does physical layout and the formal organizational structure. However, the team that is in charge of the merger decides how to use each of these integration levers, and that's where responsibility ultimately lies.

The team responsible for merger integration is tasked with developing the processes and plans around combining the two companies. As with other teams, a number of issues can emerge in terms of communication patterns. One person can dominate the conversation, people can interrupt each other, and so on. In M&A these problems are magnified, because the two organizations can have radically different cultures.

Some companies, for example, could have strong social norms around group debate, encouraging people to speak out when they don't agree. Other companies prefer to air disagreements in private, only discussing general ideas when in larger groups. If these two companies merge, their cultural differences could easily start them off on the wrong foot. This means that merger integration teams must be extremely sensitive to these differences. Before substantive discussions take place, frank and open discussion must occur about how each company operates. Having this open communication might seem like common sense, but cultural difference problems destroy group dynamics with surprising frequency.

This issue is best illustrated in a study we did using the Sociometric Badges in a collaborative engineering project with student groups from different countries. These groups of between 8 and 10 were responsible for building a Rube Goldberg machine, which would be judged by a panel of experts. The winning machine would then be placed in a prestigious science museum in Tokyo. Participants wore the Sociometric Badges throughout the week-long exercise, and groups received daily feedback from the badges on their communication patterns. Importantly, the groups were made up of both American and Japanese students, some of whom did not have a high level of English proficiency. As you might expect, this made communication difficult, even though the groups each had two facilitators who were fluent in both Japanese and English.

As the exercise went on, however, group dynamics gradually improved. After seeing their feedback, the American students realized that they needed to slow down and try to elicit more communication from their Japanese counterparts, and the Japanese students saw that they needed to speak up more. By the end of the week, the groups were collaborating extremely well.

Figure 8.1 illustrates how communication patterns changed for one of the groups. Each circle represents a participant, with the size of the circle indicating total speaking time. The color shows the interactivity level for each participant (black = interactive, white = lecture style). Interactivity here is defined as the amount of time a person speaks before someone else starts speaking. The lines represent turn taking—in other words who speaks after whom.

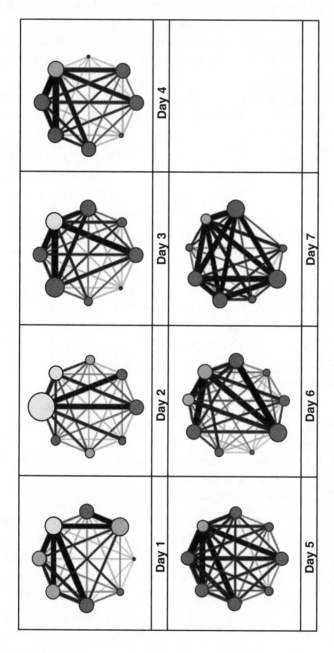

Figure 8.1 Collaboration dynamics for an international student group

As you can see from Figure 8.1, on the first day the two Japanese students are barely participating (the two lower-left circles), and there is a strong clique of American students (four top circles). These dynamics persist for a day or two, but gradually they start to change. By the end of the event, it's clear that the students are all very interactive, participating frequently, and not engaging in the sort of cliqueish behavior that occurred at the beginning. The facilitators (the two lower-right circles) are also barely participating, which is a huge positive. We went on to validate these results in laboratory experiments, even giving feedback in real time to show how data from the badges could be used to seamlessly alter conversational dynamics in positive ways.

For merger integration teams, the message couldn't be clearer. These teams often don't have a common language, relying on translators to get the job done. But as illustrated by the study, that might not be enough. Even when these groups do speak the same language, each organization has its own communication styles that could wreak havoc on the delicate, complicated process of merger integration.

However, some companies have gotten good at M&A precisely because they pay attention to these issues. Google, for example, goes through dozens of acquisitions a year, and it has a great M&A track record, with an acquisition success rate of more than 60%.[6] Part of this success is due to its strong commitment to culture and its integration process, while another factor is its reliance on data to drive internal company dynamics.

You might not be surprised that when it comes to applying data to these issues, Google is at the forefront. They have a human resources division unlike any in the industry. Dubbed "People Analytics," (I approve of the title) this group is made up of PhDs from top management schools, former consultants, and programmers. This background helps them apply an experimental and data-driven approach to company culture.

The People Analytics team analyzes internal e-mail communication patterns to try to understand how information flows within Google. It experiments with benefits, changing the way that some people are paid or the type of food they have available. It uses dozens of surveys sent out over the course of the year to see how these changes affect job satisfaction and performance. It even has a yearly survey called Googlegeist that assesses the engagement and happiness of Google's workforce.

The results speak for themselves. Google is able to recruit the best and the brightest talent, and in 2012 it was ranked as the best place to work by Fortune[7] (as well as in 2007 and 2008). Today it has grown into an Internet juggernaut with a higher market capitalization than Coca-Cola.

Google's success, however, isn't so easy to transfer to other companies. It has an HR group full of top-flight management PhDs and employees who are willing to devote a lot of their time so HR can collect data. This software company is also not averse to rapid experimentation, which is something that would be a bit more difficult to implement in, say, a major financial institution.

With access to even more data streams from devices such as the Sociometric Badge, however, companies can apply the Google approach in other industries and even improve on it. By putting a strong emphasis on culture and making use of electronic communication data, Google is able to cut the typical M&A failure rate by about 50%. Now imagine adding Sociometric Badges to that equation. Suddenly there is a good chance to lower M&A failure to more reasonable levels, to use data to fundamentally reshape the M&A process.

The math is pretty simple. Bad M&A deals lead to losses of $1.2 trillion a year. E-mail data is free, and even if every year companies bought sensors for every employee involved in M&A anywhere in the world, they would still come out with about 99.9% of the savings over the current miserable M&A performance. To deal with the ever-increasing complexity of M&A, and the world in general, using these sensors is a no brainer.

9

Attach Bolt "A" to Plank "Q"
Matching Formal Dependencies with Informal Networks

Everything today is more complex than it was yesterday. Things just keep getting bigger, better, and more complex. It's almost like a law of nature.

This complexity makes dealing with the world a challenge. Even after people master a task, something new gets added on or a new device comes out that makes what we have obsolete, forcing us to change. We have to be constantly learning, adapting, and coordinating to make sure we're on the right track.

Things get more complex because the knowledge that we acquire becomes embedded in the things we make. After we realize how to get two computers to wirelessly communicate, for example, that functionality becomes embedded in every computer. We build on top of that, and now that functionality is an inseparable part of that product.

Unfortunately, people still have to know how all of those fundamental parts work. Someone must understand how to make that part, what it needs to work properly, and how to make it better. Think of a computer. The major systems that make up a computer are a screen, a keyboard, a hard drive, a motherboard, and an operating system.

When you buy a computer from Dell or HP, you buy this complete package. But Dell doesn't actually make the vast majority of the computer's parts. Dell has gotten good at putting those parts together, but each individual part is made by a different manufacturer. There are hard drive manufacturers, operating system developers, processor manufacturers, and so on.

Taking the hard drive as an example, you can see that it's actually made up of many subcomponents. Hard disk drives are composed of magnetic platters that are encoded by a magnetic *write head* with the data you want to store. The write head looks kind of like the stylus on record players. The disks spin incredibly fast, up to 14400 RPM, and the write head moves at equivalent speeds. For all of this to work you need a processor to control the write head, a motor to spin the platters at particular speeds, and the actual platters themselves. Hard drive companies don't necessarily make any of these components themselves, but instead contract out the individual parts to third parties.

Following the chain down to the write head controller, you arrive at a computer chip company that manufactures these processors. These smaller processors are composed of a variety of circuits that create memory and calculation capabilities. These are typically all designed in house, so this is one end of the chain, right? Not yet! This company has to actually acquire raw materials, which means that they need suppliers for the silicon, copper, and other materials that they use. This normally requires the company to contract with a distributer, who will in turn have contracts with mining companies who actually dig up or chemically create the raw materials.

All of that complexity was just one path down the chain of production for a commonplace product. There are millions of these chains, which lead to networks touching millions upon millions of people.

So projects today are big. Really big. I mean really, *really* big. Small businesses that make furniture or craft goods from scratch still exist, but these products take months or years to produce and can only be manufactured on a small scale. The massive chains of production just discussed touch people from all parts of the world in all walks of life, and it's clear that the drivers of the world economy are these big projects.

Building computers is relatively simple compared to some of the projects going on in the world today. These projects take place over even larger scales and have an even bigger economic impact, but they're also prone to many different problems.

Take, for example, Boeing's 787 Dreamliner, their airplane released in 2011. That plane has hundreds of thousands of parts. Every single one of these parts has to be designed, tested, and manufactured individually. After these parts are assembled into an individual airplane system, which also has to be designed, they have to be thoroughly tested again. When all the systems are put together to make a complete airplane, everything needs to be tested once again.

Boeing had 50 teams from 44 companies in 10 countries working to get the 787 off the ground. This feat requires a massive coordination effort, and positively dwarfs the organization of plane production only 40 years ago. In 1969 Boeing took 16 months to produce the first 747. The 787 took more than 6 years (2 years longer than originally estimated) and cost $32 billion.

The 787 is undoubtedly more complex than the 747. Its fuselage is made of cutting-edge materials, it is 20% more fuel efficient than the comparable 767,[1] and a number of technological improvements make the cabin quieter and much more hospitable than in previous airplanes.

It's no coincidence that the incredibly complex 787 started experiencing problems only a few years after it first took to the skies. A serious battery fire, in addition to other problems, grounded 787s across the world in early 2013. Although the exact cause has yet to be revealed, the root of these problems can be traced to the complex dependencies between technological systems.

Projects have gotten more complex because our power to execute them has increased dramatically over time. The Internet, computers, ubiquitous air travel, all have radically changed what's possible. That's not to say that there weren't massively complex projects before. Early examples such as the pyramids at Giza are monuments to the coordinated efforts of tens of thousands of individuals.

Previously, however, the interfaces between pieces in a project were much easier to define. When you build a pyramid, one brick goes on top of the other. Done. No changing requirements, no third party that you have to negotiate with, just put brick 1 on brick 2. Things gradually got more complex, with new technology incorporating an increasing number of innovations to become more effective.

Complexity really started to take off in the industrial revolution. At that time, companies manufactured steam engines, locomotives, and rifles on a large scale. These machines were an order of magnitude more complicated than what had come before, and required involved processes to manufacture them correctly. The concept of an assembly line developed, enabling rapid production of complex parts and machines.

Things changed by another order of magnitude in the modern era. No single person can make most of our complex devices by hand. In fact, no single person can make the devices that make our devices by hand.

This dependence on others makes coordination extremely difficult, and leaves traditional management techniques floundering.

We like to deal with complexity by making a comprehensive plan that everyone can follow. This lets us spend a lot of time upfront deciding how things should be and then executing it without the need to talk to each other. This was a fine way to do things when employees mostly worked on building cabinets or even clocks, where outside concerns were minimal and requirements didn't change much over the course of the project.

Today, things are constantly changing, and sometimes these complex systems just don't work the way they're supposed to. This leads teams to change their approach as well as the parameters of their system. When they don't communicate with the teams whose work depends on their own, bugs will invariably pop up.

Computer errors are a perfect example. Too many of us have had the experience of working on something only to be jarred out of reverie by a frozen computer. One reason computers freeze is that a single application doesn't understand what other applications are doing on the computer. If one application has control of file A and needs access to file B, it will ask for control of that file. If at the same time a different program controls file B and needs access to file A, the computer enters a state where neither program can run. Although this example is an oversimplification of what's actually going on, this same lack of perspective and coordination occurs in many projects today.

Big Projects, Big Problems

All of this complexity makes it easy for problems to pop up unexpectedly. These problems have a drastic impact, because a small delay in development and production could mean billions of dollars in lost revenue and extra expense for a company. Manuel Sosa, a professor at INSEAD, investigated this problem in the case of jet engines.[2]

The jet engine project that Sosa and his colleagues studied was quite complex. The engine itself was composed of eight subsystems and had a total of 54 engine components. One team was assigned to each engine component, and six additional teams were tasked with integrating these components into the overall engine.

Although these teams all had formal plans for how they would execute this project, they hadn't considered explicitly managing the interfaces between these different components. The researchers asked the teams to identify all of these interfaces to understand what the coordination requirements were.

In the next step researchers asked people whom they would communicate with over the course of the project. Although this is a survey-based method, researchers were asking about future interactions. If badge data had been available, they certainly could have examined who normally talks to each other to get a sense for where the bugs were going to pop up. Later sections discuss this topic in more detail, but there is definitely an opportunity to enhance this survey method with behavioral data.

Next they looked at where the gaps were. Specifically, they identified areas where many dependencies existed between teams but no planned communication was identified. These gaps represented potential problem areas and needed to be dealt with to avoid any problems with development, but their causes are complex.

Organizational boundaries are a major source of collaborative discord and the gaps discussed above. Almost by definition, if you don't report to someone, then you don't have to communicate with him. Unless you go out of your way to communicate with him to talk about a dependency, a gap will result. Although formal structures are a blunt instrument for enforcing collaboration across boundaries, because your salary depends on effective communication with your bosses, you can bet that you'll make the effort to talk with them.

Of course, speaking with someone is difficult if you're not in the same place. This is often the case with teams working on complex projects, because if a team is composed of hundreds of people, then co-locating them is often difficult. Even if teams are on the same campus, they are normally on separate floors or in separate buildings. As discussed in Chapter 4, this setup makes it unlikely that they will ever talk to each other.

The boundary problem can be attacked in a few ways. Creating new reporting relationships is certainly one way to go, and this approach is favored in many organizations.

Assigning a team to specifically coordinate interfaces between teams can also be effective. This is almost like a light form of matrixing, where some formal processes are in place for reporting to these integration teams. Using these teams might be preferable to modifying the org chart, however, because they are explicitly formed to coordinate and facilitate communication rather than to order around.

For these coordination teams to be effective, they need to be able to easily communicate with all teams involved, and that means they need face-to-face communication. For issues as complex as jet engine construction or computer chip design, rich communication channels are needed to keep everyone on the same page. Whether or not a company uses coordination teams, getting people in the same place at least part of the time is important.

As discussed in Chapter 4, research shows that the more time teams spend together in person, the better they perform. However, keeping the amount of travel reasonable is important. There are simply diminishing returns as these different teams meet more frequently, because eventually people will be spending most of their time traveling. They won't have time to get anything done. Still, the $25,000 spent on a few dozen plane tickets saves millions of dollars on extra labor and time lost. Truly a no-brainer.

These priorities matter not just for financial considerations, but also for how communication time is allocated. Although the tendency is to focus most of our time concentrating on the hard problems, the interfaces that require a lot of coordination, too often the small stuff slips through the cracks. When Sosa and his colleagues looked at how people wanted to spend their time, they typically ignored communicating with teams who were working on non-critical interfaces.

Problems arise when these high-priority problems become employees' sole focus. By not spending a little time touching base with people on routine interfaces, you can bet that those interfaces will soon become far from routine if something changes.

A good analogy is how the Massachusetts Bay Transportation Authority (MBTA) deals with the crumbling state of its subway system. When it was first built in the late 1800s, the subway system was a technological marvel, the first active subway in the United States. The system has expanded over time to cover most of the greater Boston metro area, and is the main mode of transportation for about 30% of Boston's commuters.

Over time the subway system fell into disrepair. With a massive load of debt hoisted on it by the state, the MBTA was faced with some harsh budgetary realities. It could fix critical problems and ignore the less-urgent ones, or it could take on a small amount of additional debt and fix the non-critical problems as well. It opted to focus solely on critical problems, and the result has been financial catastrophe. The MBTA has been forced to take loans against future revenue streams to pay for its yearly upkeep, and it is constantly on the precipice of going bankrupt. The situation is so bad that the MBTA actually employs blacksmiths to forge train parts that aren't made anymore.[3]

The issue with the MBTA's approach is that when you ignore one of these small problems for a few years, all of a sudden it becomes a critical problem. These problems then cost far more to fix. Because the MBTA does not have the funds to adequately deal with its problems, it falls further into debt. This is many times the debt it would have incurred if it had taken the up-front cost of fixing these smaller problems, but the focus on only critical issues obscured the long-term objective.

The general problem with how people prioritize in big projects is the tendency to focus on the big things and ignore the small stuff until they become big things. This is precisely where informal communication is critical. These small things aren't going to come up in formal meetings because they're not important enough to take everyone's time. But they are important enough for a chat around the water cooler, and communicating information about these smaller issues will enable the company to head off future problems well before they occur.

This again indicates the importance of enabling informal communication between teams, whether it be through cultural or workplace interventions or communication tools that facilitate discussion. In general, however, the communication tools available today are not very good at this. Internal instant messaging programs and social networking services such as Yammer, which is like an internal Twitter for companies, rely on high employee adoption and a willingness to connect with people with whom a person doesn't normally communicate. That's hard to achieve, and a challenge most of these technologies don't directly address.

This communication is also critical for checking our common assumptions, which are another major cause of coordination headaches. We often make assumptions about how to proceed on a project based on what we've done in the past, assuming that everyone is on the same page. In projects that span millions of individuals with many different backgrounds who work on hundreds of different projects at the same time, this assumption is more often than not incorrect.

These assumptions can also pop up when people rely too heavily on standards. At the start of a project, team leaders will spend time planning and designing the overall structure of the final product. Eventually these specifications will get more and more precise, until they describe in detailed language how each component interface is expected to behave.

The problem is that components often don't behave as expected. Unforeseen difficulties can force a team to modify component specifications, and strategic changes from the top can leave teams struggling to adapt their plans. Whenever these changes happen, the potential for error is introduced. While others are continuing their work and assuming that the old specifications still apply, other teams have completely changed their expectations and are working down another path.

As Chapter 3 touched on, one of the major benefits of a cohesive face-to-face network is the ability to build a common language and a common set of assumptions. In these larger projects, scale prevents that from happening. Having a cohesive group of 300 people, let alone one million people, is just not possible. This situation, however, indicates a huge opportunity for incorporating badge data into the larger organizational process, particularly when companies can pair this data with information from databases on dependencies in software and engineering systems.

Congruence, Distance, and Software

Software development is the king of dependencies. Unlike physical systems such as an airplane, there is no real limit on software complexity. Whereas planes are ultimately limited by how much stuff can be crammed into an airframe, a program is only limited by how big people's hard drives are. A typical program involves a continuously evolving set of billions of commands, and these commands interact with other parts of the computer that the software developer does not directly control. Not surprisingly, this can cause some problems.

Beyond the sheer scale of these programs, the way that they're constructed also makes coordination problems a very real possibility. At a very simplified level, a computer program is essentially a collection of modules that interact with each other. These modules can be large programs in their own right or small routines that perform the most rudimentary tasks.

Consider a simple program with two modules. One module raises a number to a power (call this POW), and the other module asks the user to input two numbers (let's call this INPUT). POW expects to receive two numbers, x and y, and then returns x^y. Suppose INPUT, however, thinks that POW will actually return y^x. This would most likely cause INPUT to completely fail or make substantial errors when it uses POW, all because two modules that depended on each other didn't know how to interact.

This example is extremely simplistic, and a straightforward problem such as this would likely be resolved quickly. In real software, however, the problems are much more nuanced, depending on the overall state of the program as well as the computer as a whole.

Given their importance, dependencies have been put center stage in the software development community. Dependency tracking tools have been incorporated into nearly all major development environments, which programmers use to create software, and for decades methods for automatically detecting dependency issues have been a hot topic in computer science.

More recently, the importance of communication has entered into this equation. Researchers and practitioners alike realized that using formal reporting tools alone didn't solve the need for interaction between programmers to ensure that dependencies are adequately covered. They even developed a terminology for these issues.

Dependencies can either be adequately covered by communication, or they can fall by the wayside. *Congruence* occurs when there is alignment between software requirements and communication patterns—that is, when there is communication between the programmers responsible for dependent code modules. In contrast, *gaps* arise when there is no communication between these programmers. Graphically, the relationships look like that shown in Figure 9.1.

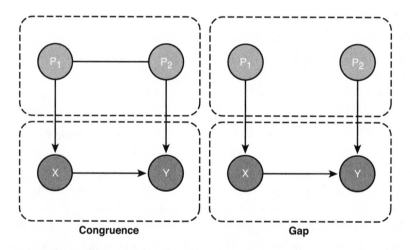

Congruence   **Gap**

Figure 9.1 Programmers, code, and dependencies

In Figure 9.1, P_1 and P_2 represent programmers, and the gray circles represent different code modules. Lines represent dependencies/responsibilities for modules. In this case, because module X depends on module Y, P_1 is the dependent and P_2 is the parent.

As you can probably infer from the earlier discussion, gaps are overwhelmingly associated with software bugs. In a landmark study, Marcelo Cataldo and his colleagues showed that congruent relationships resulted in 32% faster completion times as compared to other relationships.[4] When development cycles can stretch on for years, this represents a significant benefit of congruence.

Don't Fall into the Gap

A decade ago the data needed to investigate congruence and gaps wasn't available, but today these dependencies are exhaustively specified by programmers. This is particularly necessary in massive projects, because having to coordinate with people that one has no direct contact with is likely. By providing a standard interface that others can plug into, a programmer can let other people know how his module will react to different inputs.

Communication, however, is not necessarily a normal part of the development process. In traditional software development, dependencies and modules are assigned in the planning stages of a project, and execution proceeds assuming that programmers will faithfully reproduce this master plan. This usually doesn't happen, however, because anticipating problems that can appear during development is nearly impossible for planners. Whether the changes arise from unrealistic response time requirements, aesthetic changes that occur mid-stream, or something else, they all require coordination and communication.

Lately, development environments have incorporated communication functionality into the overall program. This often takes the form of comment fields and instant messaging channels that developers can associate with particular pieces of code.

These tools have become even more crucial to use as developers are increasingly spread over larger and larger distances. Due to its perceived formality and the availability of cheap labor with equivalent skill sets in developing countries, software development is probably the most distributed white-collar profession.

Unfortunately, development across multiple locations has been associated with project delays and increased work for individual employees. This mostly results from the lack of face-to-face communication and differences in time zone, which makes having rich interactions with other people on the team difficult. These communication effects would, presumably, affect the prevalence of congruence and gaps.

Along with Kate Ehrlich and Mary Helander from IBM, I investigated precisely how co-located and distributed teams collaborate and how this communication related to gaps.[5] By collecting a rich data set not just on communication, but on the dependencies between different code modules, we were able to discover a number of ways that both co-located and distributed teams could improve their coordination.

In this project we examined a medium-sized development team of 161 programmers working across 20 sub-teams. Some people were on multiple teams, and some of the teams were co-located, whereas others spanned multiple locations. Importantly, all team members used English as their primary language.

These teams heavily utilized a software development environment that recorded data on code dependencies as well as provided communication tools for people to comment on pieces of code or directly with each other. We scraped this data from the development environment, in total obtaining records on thousands of dependencies and tens of thousands of comments.

Overall, the average programmer had code that depended on 32.5 other modules in the project, with a high of 177 dependencies. Even the average number of dependencies is a lot to keep track of, especially because each of these dependencies can change at any time. While not all of these dependencies are crucial, it often falls on the dependent to make sure that none of his interfaces with other modules has changed. This makes sense, because someone working on a critical module would have a hard time satisfying the requirements for the 100 or so modules that depend on it. However, it does mean that dependents need to keep on their toes.

A look at the breakdown of congruency and gaps revealed what we might expect. Gaps were much more common when dependencies spanned groups in different locations. In general much of the work in this group was done remotely, so there were actually 22% more dependencies in remote teams. Figure 9.2 illustrates the results.

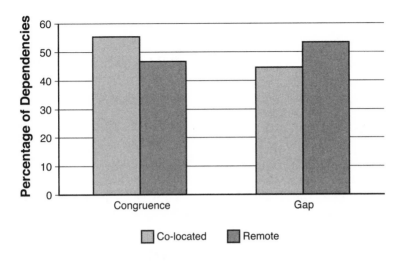

Figure 9.2 Congruencies and gaps by programmer location

For co-located groups, about 55% of all dependencies were congruent, whereas there were gaps for 45% of dependencies. Remote groups essentially flipped these numbers, with 47% congruencies and 53% gaps. This is an extremely large difference. These results imply that remote programming groups are 8% less effective than co-located groups. Also remember that in this case everyone's native language was English. What would have happened if some of the groups had difficulty communicating in the lingua franca of the other groups?

To calculate the presence or absence of a gap, however, the study only examined whether there was *any* communication between the two parties relating to the dependency. As you might imagine, a single comment probably indicates a low level of coordination, whereas a high number of comments indicates that people are actively engaged in addressing potential issues. Because this is all electronic communication, nothing is physically preventing people from communicating. However, the numbers are pretty overwhelming.

The average dependency for remote groups received 8.4 comments. Co-located dependencies, on the other hand, had an average of 38.1 comments. In this team, face-to-face communication clearly bolsters the overall level of collaboration between coworkers. This enables them to not only address dependencies with more regularity than their remote colleagues, but also to address them more effectively.

Keeping in Contact

The importance of congruence and gaps is impossible to overlook. Gaps have an overwhelmingly negative impact on performance by increasing bugs and slowing development time by more than 30%. This serious issue spans across many of the world's fastest-growing fields such as vehicle development, programming, and complex engineering projects. Making sure these groups address their dependency problems is critical for their success.

As these projects grow in scale, having everyone working on them in the same place can become infeasible. As the study results show, this is potentially a major issue. Teams working remotely need to place an even greater emphasis on achieving congruence, and using lightweight digital communication tools alone might not be enough.

Collaborators need to actively set up video conferences, phone calls, and chat sessions to make sure that these dependencies are being addressed. Although this extra communication takes time out of the workday, spending an extra 5% of one's time talking with collaborators versus an extra 30% of one's time debugging seems clear-cut.

Organizations can also work to assign "brokers" who will actively try to connect distributed groups. These brokers are ideally people who travel frequently to different locations or are at least in close contact with relevant stakeholders. Their informal sense of who should be talking to whom and making the act of connection a part of their daily routine will pay huge dividends for the organization in the medium and long term. These introductions create congruence, which speeds development time for a particular project and creates relationships that span distance and organizational boundaries. As the examples in this book have illustrated, those relationships are the glue that holds companies together.

A last important note is that dependencies need to be matched by the physical layout of the workplace. Chapter 4 covered how distance is an important driver of communication; that result emerged at a different level in this project, which showed in striking relief the added importance of dependencies. By mashing these two findings together, companies can accurately choose an ideal workplace layout.

When companies decide which teams sit where and even what cities teams are located in, dependencies need to be a major consideration. Although at the outset of a project knowing what dependencies will emerge and who will be responsible for which modules might be difficult, the general structure should be relatively clear. This allows companies to strategically choose team locations to drastically reduce the prevalence of gaps using the power of serendipity. In this case bumping into other people in the hallway or at the coffee area has an immediate impact on performance by helping people coordinate their work, to speak nothing of the long-term benefits of these interactions.

I don't want to imply that teams need to constantly move desks or transfer to different cities as their short-term dependencies change. That would be a logistical nightmare and end up costing an inordinate amount of time and peace of mind for employees. The major point is that organizational strategy at the macro level and dependencies at the micro level need to be manifested in the design of the workplace. Companies must strive to make this critical face-to-face communication as likely as possible, because as the study results emphasized, digital tools can't be relied on to bridge the gap.

If companies' collaboration methods don't change, projects such as the Dreamliner are going to get even longer and more expensive. In about 40 years Boeing went from making a new plane in 16 months to 120 months. Even at a much slower rate of change, in another 40 years it would take a company such as Boeing well over a decade and cost hundreds of billions of dollars to develop a new aircraft. Something has to change. The primary time sink in these projects is the need for congruency. Making changes such as the ones suggested in this chapter can effectively reverse this trend. That's not to say that Boeing's next aircraft will take 16 months to produce, but it could.

10

The Future of Organizations
How People Analytics
Will Transform Work

The modern organization is truly amazing. Thousands of years ago, humanity could do little more than produce a few simple sailing vessels, rudimentary weapons, and singular artifacts. Some of the organizations that produced these items, however, consisted of hundreds or even thousands of individuals.

Eventually, humanity gave birth to the formal field of management, which tries to guide the development of products and services under a more scientific framework. Companies have continually accelerated the process and scale of development. Emerging from that vast tidal wave of history and evolution and accident, the wave that finally touches the shore is the modern organization.

Over the last few decades, information technology has had a major impact on organizational design. By changing how people communicate, IT has enabled companies to consider new ways to collaborate at work. Before the Internet, collaborating on a document with a team in another city was unthinkable. Because experts can be anywhere in the world, however, collaboration through e-mail became a desirable option. The rise of mobile telephony and real-time video chat enabled companies to open extremely small branches all over the world, further relying on local expertise and rapid, rich communication between different teams.

Certainly, further advances in IT will occur, and they will have similarly profound impacts on the way people organize, but none of these tools are reflective. That is, they don't feed anything directly back into the organization.

Think of a company as a water system. The formal and informal parts of the organization are like the pipes. Some pipes come from informal processes such as bumping into people around the coffee machine, whereas other pipes represent formal reporting relationships. If you can structure the pipes correctly, the right amount of water will end up getting to the right destination. Otherwise, you'll burst a faucet in a house in Kentucky because you routed all the water for the state of New York to a small outlet, while other parts of the country experience widespread drought because you siphoned off too much water.

IT is like the pump. The better it performs, the faster it can push water around the pipes, and the quicker you can adjust to any change that emerges at the ends of the system. Better pumps might also lead you to build new pipes and remove old ones to take advantage of the additional pressure and speed that the new pump affords.

However, the pump will never tell you whether you laid your pipes correctly in the first place. Companies today have a very good understanding of the pump and what comes out at the end of the different pipes, but they have no idea what's going on inside of those pipes. This is where the next frontier of management lies: in using sensing to change organizations.

What this book has covered is how sensing technology, and big data about organizations in general, can have massive effects on the way companies are organized. From changing the org chart to changing coffee areas, no aspect of organizations will be untouched by the widespread application of this data.

Because this technology is so new, the scope of the studies examined in this book has been limited to single companies. I hope that by expounding on some of the general lessons from these projects, I've been able to convince you of the transformative power of data, particularly communication data. This work will expand in the future—already dozens of research groups around the world are applying this sensing methodology in their work.

Imagine, however, that in the future Sociometric Badges and the other methods you have seen used in this book aren't just limited to a few companies and some academic projects. What if the Sociometric Badge became everyone's ID card? What if instead of thousands of people wearing badges, millions of people were wearing badges continuously for decades? What things could we learn about how to better manage companies? What new opportunities would arise?

Badges, Badges Everywhere?

Before getting carried away by possibilities, a couple issues need to be addressed. Is this vision of long-term, widespread badge use actually feasible? Will people really wear badges that can track their behavior all the time? For it to become a reality, two things are necessary: ease of use and privacy protections.

Ease of use is relatively simple to tackle, because electronics are always getting smaller, cheaper, and faster. Most company ID badges already have an RFID chip inside, which is essentially a very cheap sensor. Even the current version of the Sociometric Badge is getting close to these ID cards in size and weight, with the battery remaining the biggest bottleneck to further miniaturization.

Using sensors and calculating voice features takes power. This is why your cell phone runs out of juice more quickly when you turn on Bluetooth and GPS. When you transmit a signal over the air, you're effectively blasting light waves in all directions. This is what the badge does to help detect conversations. On top of that, voice features are constantly computed when someone is speaking, requiring signal processing algorithms to run on the badge's processor. When someone isn't speaking, a lot of the processor's parts can be turned off, further saving power. The point is that all of this activity takes a lot of juice. The current version of the badges does pretty well: The battery lasts for about one work week without needing to be recharged.

Recent innovations in battery technology, from inductive charging to over-the-air power transfer, mean that in a few years the badges won't even have to be directly recharged. They can be charged simply by placing them on the table for a few minutes or even wirelessly beaming electricity from an in-office power station. With some clever engineering, the power consumption of these sensors could be reduced even further, until soon people are using these sensors as their regular ID badges.

The privacy portion of the equation, however, gets more complicated. When sensing technology becomes commonplace, the Sociometric Badge won't be the only option. Other companies could make similar devices with similar capabilities, but instead of adhering to a participant-centered version of privacy as discussed in Chapter 1, some of them would likely have a different approach. If the badges are now your ID, after all, will people still have to opt-in to data collection, or would companies turn it on by default?

These questions are difficult to answer and indicate that strict legal mechanisms must be in place to ensure that companies don't have access to individual data. Although pockets in the legal community that are interested in establishing such standards exist, such as the Berkman Center for Internet and Society at Harvard, this movement is only slowly gaining traction. Without these protections, sensing technology could create a poisonous work environment, one in which people are constantly worried about being spied on and monitored down to the tiniest movement.

This type of environment completely defeats the purpose of the badges and organizational sensing in general. The badges are designed to help make people happier and more productive, things that all companies should strive for. There's just not a good business case for checking what Bob was doing at 2:30 p.m. on Tuesday. Not only is exposing that information a huge violation of privacy, it also wastes the company's time. The things that all companies should care about are

- What makes people in this company productive and happy?
- How can the company change to make people happier and more productive?

Notice there is nothing about individuals, because that data is too specific to affect broad change across an organization.

The issue of privacy deserves a book in and of itself, so not a lot of time can be spent on it here. Luckily, some great work by the World Economic Forum, *Personal Data: The Emergence of a New Asset Class*,[1] outlines the challenges in this space and describes in detail the framework that needs to be in place for innovation to continue.

It's heartening that governments and businesses at such high levels are paying attention to this issue and agree on the basic "new deal on data" principles.

You should feel more confident that not only will technology such as the Sociometric Badges become widespread, but it will also be adopted in a privacy-preserving fashion. So what will happen after millions of devices are scattered across the globe? Let's take a tour of what this would look like, from integrating new employees to the fundamental building blocks of management.

Moving Toward the People Analytics System

Imagining the benefits of deploying badges across a Fortune 500 company with hundreds of thousands of employees is easy. In all the projects discussed in this book, researchers used natural variation in the way that people work and communicate to identify the things that make people effective and happy. After isolating these effects, organizational leaders can bring those lessons to the rest of the company in the form of a *people analytics system*.

Having hundreds of thousands of employees at the same company wear badges for years on end can multiply these benefits. Every facet of the organization can be analyzed and modified to be more effective. Although this book discusses many of those areas, these changes could be made at an even larger scale.

Let's now begin where all companies do: hiring employees. Onboarding new hires is one of the most difficult things that companies have to do, with the common statistic being that bringing on a new employee costs about 25% of that employee's salary. Using the badges, however, could affect this process at a basic level.

Consider training employees at a retail store. They have to learn the culture of the organization, how to restock the shelves, how to work the cash register, and how to interact with customers. Sensors could be injected into every part of this equation. Reading RFID tags on clothing could help employees track their restocking speed (this technology is already used at many warehousing facilities), and cash registers could time transactions to give feedback on speed and errors.

The big payoff, however, would be in cultural integration and customer interaction. On the culture side, employees could look at how integrated they are in the social fabric of the organization. This would show how cohesive their group was, and the people analytics system would automatically suggest ways that they could change their interaction patterns. For example, if they're eating lunch alone, then going out to lunch with some of their colleagues might help build cohesiveness. This data could also find its way into shift scheduling, so that the right people are paired up with each other when they're taking inventory, manning the cash registers, or stocking shelves.

Improving interaction with customers would have a direct impact on their paycheck, because employees in many stores are partially paid on commission. Learning how the most effective salespeople interact with customers, in terms of tone of voice, volume, and speaking speed, would all be extremely helpful to new and veteran employees. Employees could work on voice pitch in real time by talking to the computer to gauge their speaking style, or look at feedback reports afterward to check their progress.

At its core, showing employee progress and disseminating best practices automatically would be a huge contribution of the people analytics system. Today these practices occur through an arduous process of trickle-up reporting. If an employee at one store figures out an effective way to interact with a customer, it has to first be noticed by his boss, then reported up to her boss, and up and up and up until it eventually finds its way into the employee training program. After this practice is codified, however, feedback on how an employee matches up to that ideal is subjective or even non-existent. Most companies act as if employees are veterans after going through the training program, but of course there is normally a learning curve that continues for years—not to mention the fact that best practices can frequently change. If a store starts selling a new kind of product, it can take a long time for new best practices to make their way back up the hierarchy.

Beyond the individual level, communication data allows companies to look at how people work together and how to help them do that effectively. Even before putting a team together, however, companies could simulate how well they can expect employees to work together and what challenges are likely to emerge. As discussed in Chapter 3, communication dynamics are the lifeblood for team success. Some projects need a group with diverse connections to gather new information quickly, whereas other projects need tight-knit connections to execute tasks effectively. Companies could test out different team configurations beforehand to maximize these different traits and be more confident of their success. Data from sensors and digital communication records would help determine what tasks different teams would be good at, creating a sort of "team fingerprint" that employers could match with certain task types.

Another important benefit of teams is that they create long-term social capital. In other words, if you work on a team with someone, you develop a deep relationship with that person. Down the line you can call on that person if you're working on another project that requires her expertise. Passing along information that's relevant to you is also easy for her, because she knows what you're interested in. Constructing a team fingerprint is then not just about how a team would perform on a specific project, but how it would benefit the company down the line. Using sensor data to drive these predictions would make the team fingerprint a major driver of organizational success.

After a team is formed, giving members a sense for how their dynamics are changing over time is also important, particularly as it relates to different phases of a project. These dynamics could even be shown at the meeting level, using a real-time feedback system to continuously tune participation dynamics over long periods of time. People who tend not to participate in meetings could be visually encouraged to jump in by seeing their participation bar flash, while people who were overly dominating discussions could also be flagged.

In fact, my colleague Taemie Kim at MIT developed an early version of this system called the Meeting Mediator. Using data from the Sociometric Badge, this system showed participation levels and communication patterns for each meeting participant, encouraging dominant individuals to pull back and less talkative people to speak up. In a number of studies, from trust games to brainstorming tasks to decision-making scenarios, Taemie was able to show that teams who used this system trusted each other more and cooperated more effectively. Imagine the kind of influence this system would have if it wasn't just used as a one-off, but became part of a team's culture.

At a more general level of communication, the people analytics system could show a team's balance between exploration (communicating with people in diverse groups) and execution (having a tightly coordinated collaboration pattern). Depending on the needs of the team at any given moment, this data could deliver suggestions for how to shift this balance as well as make slight modifications to the work environment.

Teams that are actively trying to gather new information, for example, might be encouraged to ask for introductions from certain colleagues. The system could even start sending invitations for social events that other groups are holding if the data says this would be beneficial for all involved. The point is not to create awkward social moments where strangers show up uninvited, but to make people aware of opportunities to meet their colleagues in new ways.

With this proactive and intuitive organization, the formal org chart will rapidly fade in importance. Although in the past the org chart was useful to help channel communication and collaboration, with widespread adoption of sensing technology and communication data mining, the focus will change to creating an environment that nurtures the connections between people. To make this idea more concrete, imagine a company wants to open a new line of business. Previously this would involve creating an org chart, spending months figuring out who would fill out that organization, and developing a strategic plan to guide the new division.

That strategic piece will likely remain, but now imagine that this sensing-based organizational dashboard is deployed across the company. The people analytics system observed many new divisions open up over time, and has seen what factors lead to success from a collaborative perspective. After the basic team functions for the project are chosen, the system would know with a high level of accuracy how the different teams should be connected, how the teams should collaborate internally over the course of the project, and what factors allow those effective communication patterns to flourish. More importantly, this could also change over time. Rather than having a set org chart, collaboration patterns could rapidly change depending on issues that arise during the project.

You've already learned about some ways to affect communication patterns, but let's figure out how these would all connect to the people analytics system. One lever at our disposal is the physical office layout. As goals change, the system will know the office layout, in terms of social areas, furniture, and desk location, that will best achieve those goals. Coffee area and café locations are important drivers of collaboration. Desk location and even the type of cubicle people are in, as you saw in Chapter 4, often influence who people talk to more than any formal requirements. Clearly, ripping out old cubicles and putting in new ones every week, or even every few months, is impractical. Coffee machines, however, are easily moved. Desks can also be changed every few months without much interruption, especially if they are on wheels.

Imagine that on Monday the system sends out an e-mail to a team member suggesting a new location for the coffee machine. Walking through the office in the morning and seeing the coffee machine cart migrating to its new home could become a normal sight. Imagining a "moving day" where people across the office spend a few hours swapping seats in a semi-chaotic game of musical chairs is also not difficult. This practice is actually not so different from what happens in offices today. Offices are frequently reorganized based on changing constraints. The difference is that with the people analytics system, data drives those changes, making internal migration a part of the corporate culture.

In offices with open seating, we don't even have to encourage internal migration. People already choose their desks every day, although normally their choices are based on gut instinct. The people analytics system could sit on top of this process and send everyone seating suggestions in the morning to optimize collaboration patterns. People could still choose whatever seat they wanted, but now they could use hard data to make their decisions.

The sensing technology can also be incorporated into the environment itself. As an experimental project at MIT, Alex Speltz and I developed what we called an "augmented cubicle." The cubicle itself had the same dimensions as a standard cubicle wall, but instead of being lined with beige fabric it was composed of a window shade sandwiched between two panes of plexiglass. The window shade was connected via a wire to a small motor in the base of the cubicle wall, which was in turn connected to a small computer that we could communicate with over Wi-Fi.

The motivation for building this wall was to make people more or less visible to others based on their social context. So if it seemed like one group in the office needed to talk more with another group based on project dependencies or long-term social capital factors, then at night a program would signal all the cubicle walls between the two groups to raise their blinds. When everyone came in the next day, you could walk by someone's desk and easily see what they were doing and seamlessly start chatting with them. Of course, a manual option would be available to move the shade up or down when workers didn't want to be disturbed, but in general most people stick with defaults.

The shades wouldn't change more than once or twice a week, and they would only move at night. This practice would preserve a natural office environment while taking advantage of the rapid changes possible via a people analytics system and a bunch of motors. This concept might seem like one that's far down the line, but the idea that an office could be reactive to its inhabitants in a non-intrusive way is a powerful one. Most likely this approach will start working its way into all of our lives in the not-too-distant future.

Another lever to consider is communication tools. This book has examined some of the ways people can communicate today, but new channels are constantly added to our repertoire. Internal Twitter clients such as Yammer have started to gain in popularity, and consumer tools such as Google Hangouts are quickly making their way into the corporate world as well. Add these onto face-to-face, phone, IM, chatrooms (which are still refusing to go away), discussion boards, teleconferences, and wikis, and the number of communication channels starts to look overwhelming.

This extreme power of choice is not necessarily a good thing. If you work at a company where different groups use all of these different tools, then you might find it impossible to talk to each other. The marketing group might be composed of heavy IM users, for instance, while the finance people could be wiki devotees. Instead of making communication easier, the proliferation of tools can have the opposite effect.

This does not mean that more choice is always bad, or even the fact that certain groups use specialized communication tools is bad. For example, allowing software developers to communicate within their development environment makes them much more effective. It helps them coordinate with their colleagues as well as automatically recognize problem points in software projects. However, a data-driven approach is needed to help companies figure out what tools to use and how they best support different kinds of interaction. By plugging a people analytics system into these tools, companies could roll out new tools across the organization according to communication needs or move people to more effective media by merging other tools.

A people analytics system could also be used to modify how the tools themselves actually work. In a project that I did while I was working in Japan, your relationship to the sender would actually change how e-mail was displayed. For example, if increasing the diversity of your connections would be helpful for you, then e-mails from people in other social groups would increase in size, literally standing out from all the other mail in your inbox. This slight visual nudge would be a reminder that reaching out to those other people might be a good idea.

This feature doesn't just apply to e-mail; it could also be used to display people differently in chat windows and discussion boards. Teleconferences could be similarly altered by encouraging people who aren't speaking to participate by amplifying their handset volume or ratcheting down the volume of others. These changes wouldn't force a change in behavior by itself, but would help push individuals and teams to slightly alter their communication in positive ways.

The people analytics system could also send messages over these communication channels to shape the social structure of the organization. Some general parameters might exist for how connected the company should be—that is, how many hops in the social network it takes to get from one team to another. What if you could use a people analytics system to create those ties?

Augmented Social Reality

A relatively simple way to create new relationships would be to ask for introductions, similar to what you can do on LinkedIn. The difference within an organization is that the system knows exactly whom you talk to, not just whom you explicitly connected with. The downside is that the user needs to know exactly who to talk to. For fresh perspectives or ideas, you need to talk with someone completely outside your network. Instead of cold-calling a stranger, a desirable alternative would be to have the system try to make those connections for you.

The basic concept here is fairly straightforward: Let's say I want to connect two people, and they have a friend in common. The best way to connect them would be to contact their common friend and say: "It seems like it would be helpful for your friends if you introduced them."

This method has a couple benefits over directly connecting these two people:

- The system would have a hard time figuring out whether the two friends would really hit it off (a lot of variables go into that); however, the common friend knows both of them, and probably has a good idea about their compatibility.

- To the people being introduced, having a common friend make the introductions seems like a natural social process. Friends get introduced all the time. There's just a little bit of data getting injected into the process.

This whole concept is called *Augmented Social Reality*. *Augmented Reality* refers to a field of wearable computing where programs overlay information onto video images from your phone or through special glasses. This practice has become popularized through augmented reality apps such as Layar, which you can use to see nearby tweets or the Yelp rating of restaurants, all layered on top of the live videofeed from your phone's camera. Augmented *social* reality, however, is about using sensor data to turn everyone into a social connector by layering social context on top of our everyday interactions.

Some people are just naturally good connectors, but it's an extremely difficult skill to master. By creating an augmented social reality, a layer on top of our work lives that allows us to see who we should be introducing and how to interact with people, everything flows a lot more smoothly. This framework could be used to slowly stitch together far-flung parts of the company, socially knitting them together. By going from introduction to introduction, a system could introduce one team to another that's just a bit closer to a more distant team, then making another introduction that gets them a bit closer, and so on until the teams are finally directly introduced. This process is not going to happen overnight, but making it a part of the organizational culture, a normal tool that people rely upon, could profoundly shape the network into a much more effective whole.

A people analytics system would likely find its way into other organizational processes as well. Rather than giving formal groups bonuses based on performance metrics, people from other teams who informally participated in a project could be rewarded. HR evaluations, which typically use surveys and qualitative reports from managers, would naturally benefit from an infusion of behavioral data. Organizational strategy choices could be weighted by information similarity from different team members, so that people who have a more diverse social network would have a greater voice than people who were just participating in an echo chamber. The list of applications goes on and on. In any case, one thing is clear: People analytics will radically transform the way companies do business. But for users, for workers, it will become familiar and commonplace.

All Around the World

Up to this point, the book has explored the potential of this technology within single companies. This is a relatively straightforward application of the projects that we've described, but it's also limited in scope. Each company has its own way of doing things, and this is reflected in the behavior of its employees. If you walk into an IBM office, you can quickly tell that it's not an office from Google. Similarly, the people analytics system can gather behavioral data related to employees' productivity. This approach takes advantage of the natural variation within companies of collaboration patterns and behaviors to discover the most effective (and ineffective) ways to manage people.

What about the variation between firms? IBM, for example, could try to change the way it behaves based on how Google organizes its people. Today, this type of change happens from people reading news articles, case studies, and books like this one. These are all great ways to disseminate best practices, but making the change is an incredibly slow process. It takes years before people from outside companies discover new management styles in other firms, and it can take another few years before these styles seep into the popular consciousness.

One approach to help speed up this process is to create organizational benchmarks that use data from companies all over the world. One of the most popular benchmarks in this vein is Gallup's Engagement Survey, which consists of 12 questions that they have asked to millions of people in thousands of companies all over the world. Companies participate because they want to see how they stack up against their competitors, and how they can learn from those competitors to improve on their weaknesses and capitalize on their strengths.

Now imagine this benchmarking method applied to the kind of sensor data discussed in this book. Instead of just keeping best practices within companies, lessons learned in one company can be applied to a completely different company, all in the blink of an eye. For example, suppose you've observed a hundred drug development projects at pharmaceutical companies, each with varying levels of success. You could relate that success to changes in collaboration patterns, showing that shaping a team's interactions over the course of the project can make them successful. Now whenever another pharmaceutical company starts up a project, managers know exactly what kinds of interactions to support without needing any additional input from the company.

All of this information sharing is incredibly exciting, because quickly companies in India would learn from companies in Brazil that would learn from companies in the U.S. Organizations in totally different industries with vastly different business models would be able to rapidly exchange best practices, taking advantage of similarities between their businesses inferred from hard data. The people analytics system becomes a global learning network, where the management "experts" no longer tell companies what to do, but instead the combined power of data drives how companies are organized.

This system might seem a bit scary to some managers, because it applies the same tools to management that one typically associates with automated hardware and software fixes. Management has always been a domain where soft skills are needed to make it work. This people analytics system, however, democratizes the management process.

This democratization is crucial for an area that hasn't been discussed much: small business. Companies with only a dozen or fewer people typically have very few tools at their disposal to help them manage their company. This problem is compounded by the fact that most people who open a small business have little management experience. These small businesses aren't just a sideshow in the economy, either. About half of non-farm GDP in the U.S. is generated by small businesses.

The people analytics system would essentially be "management in a box" for small businesses, enabling them to apply to their company the lessons learned from other organizations. With only a few sensors and some basic programs, people in small businesses could get automated help setting up their management structure and generating effective collaboration patterns. They could even receive feedback on their progress. Not only that, but with enough small businesses using such a system, these fledgling companies could get automated suggestions on org structure, compensation systems, and so on.

Take, for example, a bunch of friends going into business together to open an upscale pizza restaurant. They get the lease, purchase all of their cooking equipment, and finally buy their "People Analytics Starter Kit." They fire up the system, input the type of business and what each employee does, and then hand out badges to everyone. Immediately the system suggests different ways they could manage their business, from compensation systems to org charts. However, the real payoff comes when they start collecting data.

Every day the system provides automated feedback to the restaurant. It seems like the waiters have really engaging conversations with customers but tend to interact with customers less frequently than the highest performers at other establishments. It also seems like the head chef isn't checking in enough with the line cooks, which means more order errors and slower cooking times. Even in a restaurant, the chain of communication is essential to make sure that the order is going from the customer to the waiter to the head chef to the line cooks in a timely fashion. Measuring that response time and giving feedback on how to improve it could be the difference between seating 80 people for dinner and seating 100. After seeing this feedback, the waiters check on patrons every seven minutes instead of every five, and the head chef now chats with other cooks every few minutes to see what they're up to. Customers are happier, the restaurant runs better, and the results are fed back into the global system so that next new restaurant will work even better.

The Next Big Thing

The big thing is that all of this technology will be in the background. From the employee's perspective, work will look pretty much the same. The only difference is that the environment, and the organization, has been engineered in such a way that it will naturally bring out the best in people and help them enjoy work to the greatest extent possible.

A people analytics system would create a learning community of organizations the world over, not through reading articles or books, but by exchanging data. This data exchange would extend from the Walmarts of the world to the mom-and-pop stores on the corner. From companies that install augmented cubicles in hundreds of offices to businesses that just want some simple pointers, this feedback will change what it means to manage an organization. People analytics will be here to stay.

11

Where We Go from Here

Of Face-to-Face Interaction, New Collaboration Tools, and Going Back to the Future

Throughout this book, you've seen a few common threads emerge about what makes workers effective and happy in the workplace. Chief among them is the importance of face-to-face communication—specifically, cohesive face-to-face communication, where the people you talk to spend a lot of time talking with each other.

The examples in this book have shown that this communication is important for transferring complex information in an IT firm and reducing stress and increasing information flow in a call center. Having these tightly knit, face-to-face ties promotes trust and creates a common language, crucial items for today's organizations.

Having diverse ties is also helpful, as explained in Chapters 5 and 6, which cover expertise and creativity, respectively. Connecting with people from different social groups, people with access to different sources of information, helps you think of ideas that you normally wouldn't hear in the echo chamber of your tightly knit group. Organizations can help foster these ties by changing the physical office space around, rearranging breaks, and taking other small steps to nudge people in the right direction. As you saw in this book, these small nudges had very strong effects.

Despite all these revelations, let's step back and take a look at where we're going as a society. Remote work is becoming more and more common. Telecommuting is on the rise, and many people are working almost exclusively from home offices. That's partly a reflection of the times, because the flexibility people demand and the increasingly global nature of work require that we be able to work from anywhere at any time. To some extent, the new communication tools that are available support these arrangements.

We can use Skype to set up video chat with remote colleagues, use teleconferences to get everyone on the same page, or use IM programs to do some lightweight coordination. The data shows, however, that these tools aren't enough to get the job done. Part of the issue is that we evolved for millions of years to deal with people who are right in front of us. We've only had phones for 150 years, barely an eye blink of time from a evolutionary perspective. Think of how far we have to go before we biologically adapt to more recent innovations such as the Internet and instant messaging.

One of the major issues of the day is that despite our desire and need for remote communication, people are still awful at collaborating over distance. This book has already listed some simple fixes: meeting face-to-face before a project starts, spending large amounts of time working on coordination in remote groups, and so on, but this problem cries out for a new solution.

Some of the problems can be solved by injecting social context into these alien environments. Systems such as the Meeting Mediator (refer to Chapter 10 and the real-time feedback it provides are an important part of this equation. These systems help regain much of what is lost when we separate ourselves by telephone wire or blinking computer screens.

Further down the line one can easily imagine that technologies such as virtual reality and holography will come into play to directly act on the ancient mechanisms that are buried in our brains. If it looks, sounds, even smells to us like we're physically in an office with a bunch of other people, then for all intents and purposes we are. Of course, this technology has a long way to go before it becomes widely deployed, and if it is to be successful, some basic functionality will need to be supported.

One of the simplest things that throws off remote interactions is the eye gaze problem. If you've ever used Skype, you know what I'm talking about. This problem occurs because with current technology you can't look at your screen and the camera at the same time. Some solutions are out there that combat this problem with varying degrees of success. Cisco has created a TelePresence system that uses specially designed rooms and finely tuned camera and monitor placement to make it appear as if the people you're collaborating with are all sitting around a table with you. The effect is fairly striking, especially with HD cameras and a dedicated network for transmitting the video as fast as possible. The price tag, at around $300,000, however, makes this technology fairly impractical for most situations.

Other solutions, such as BiDi Screen from Matt Hirsch at MIT, take a more elegant approach. Matt developed a technology that combines a camera and a screen, so that you can look directly at the person you're talking to over a video connection. If it gets produced in mass quantities, it has the potential to be orders of magnitude cheaper than the Cisco system, but currently it's still a research project with no immediate plans for commercialization.

For now, however, let's say that this problem will be solved in time whether by BiDi Screen, TelePresence, or a similar system. One can safely say that in the next two decades this issue will become a thing of the past. Unfortunately, the biggest problem with these systems is much harder to crack and involves the fundamental design of all contemporary communication technologies. At a very basic level, in the way that every one of these systems is conceived, they are designed around planned meetings.

This isn't necessarily anyone's fault; it's just what is supportable and what designers have identified as important. This stems in large part from the enormous emphasis that has been placed on formal processes in the past hundred years. Meetings are important; talking by the coffee machine is not. So we made and continue to make better and better meeting systems, until down the line we'll come up with a system that allows us to do meetings so well over distance that we won't mind getting up at 2 a.m. for a meeting with colleagues in India (well, night owls won't mind).

However, when you look at what makes people productive, about where people really get work done, how much of that occurs within the confines of a formal meeting? Even thinking about yourself, how much of the time you spend in meetings do you feel is productive? Is that where you get your real work done? Chances are, the answer is "No."

Unfortunately, with current technology, fostering the serendipitous interactions and post-meeting socializing that forms the basis for the effectiveness of face-to-face communication is hard. There have been some attempts at addressing this problem, each with limited success. Google Hangouts is a recent foray into this area, where people leave a webcam on and invite others to come in and out as they please. There have been similar systems in the past, using always-on video, typically in common spaces, to connect workplaces in different parts of the globe.

My team at Sociometric Solutions uses Google Hangouts frequently, so I'm not going to say these systems are without merit. Right now we have people in California, Massachusetts, and Finland, so rarely is everyone able to get together in person. Even finding a time to have meetings when we're all at work is hard for us. Using Hangouts every day makes connecting when we do meet in person much easier.

Time differences, of course, can't be solved no matter how much technology you pour into the equation. Current systems are also limited in that they represent only a small window into another place, and a fairly unnatural window at that. Perhaps the solution will come when we can make screens so big with cameras of such high quality that entire walls become windows and every surface in a workplace becomes a monitor to help connect us to remote coworkers. My intuition says that it will need to be something more than that, that using social context data we could make a system that would be infinitely more subtle but no less communicative, one that visualizes social context in an intuitive way that will subtly affect our perception of other places. Time will tell.

For now, however, there needs to be an acknowledgment that face-to-face communication is critical for the complex, intensely collaborative tasks that are the lifeblood of our economy. Even when factoring in the rising cost of airfare, spending a few thousand dollars flying people to a central location is almost certainly cheaper than spending hundreds of millions of dollars on thousands of high-definition screens that will need constant maintenance and a huge IT support staff.

There is also a need to shift away from the focus on formal communication and into the informal. Indeed, informal communication is more important to a company, both from a productivity and job satisfaction perspective. This realization needs to make its way into every facet of work if we're to continue on a curve of increasing complexity. With big M&A deals and projects involving millions of workers becoming commonplace, time and again it becomes evident that the current way of doing things breaks down.

Office layout will likely lead the charge as a new area of concentration for companies. Currently, office design is relegated to an afterthought, and if management is involved in the process at all, it's usually to offer opinions on whether a particular design looks "cool." Although looks are important for a company's image and morale, an incredibly delicate dance is going on that demands close attention.

One of the issues is that choosing office space is often a political process. Bosses with good connections can typically secure the "best" space for their team, with corner offices and large desks, while politically impotent teams get stuck in the basement. Companies need to turn that process around, and instead bring a strategic approach to office design, one where political concerns take a backseat and collaborative considerations (that is, group A needs to talk to group B) drive decisions.

The problems that plague office layout are mirrored in seemingly banal furniture purchasing decisions. However, factors as ostensibly insignificant as desk length, cubicle height, and the brand of coffee machine have profound implications for collaboration. Of course, executives can't spend weeks pouring over different options, but a general directive is needed to guide furniture decisions toward high-level cultural goals. This information can filter down to individual groups so they can shape their space to fit their collaborative needs and still match the company's cultural values.

The cultural tone of a company is extremely important, and that often manifests itself in how people act during breaks. In American culture, there is a widespread belief that time not spent at your desk is time wasted, and typically people found schmoozing by the coffee machine or eating lunch at a table with colleagues are viewed with disdain. People will even spend effort to make it look like they're working.

In one office where I worked, I had a direct view into another company's space across an atrium. One of the employees was facing her computer screen, and because she was only about 30 feet away, I had a vague sense for what she was doing. I can say without exaggeration that about 90% of her time was spent watching videos on Netflix. She would get in at around 9 a.m., fire up Netflix, and proceed to watch old movies and TV shows for the entire day. Sometimes I would look up to see what movie she was watching, and I rarely saw her use another program or even get up to talk to a coworker. I guess she figured that if her boss thought she was working, everything would be okay.

People need to change this mindset. The results in this book argue that workers' most productive time occurs when they collaborate and interact with others. This means getting up and walking around, spending time in the coffee area, eating lunch with colleagues, jumping into chat sessions, and becoming heavily involved in the social life of the workplace. These cultural changes have to start with individuals, but the higher ups need to show that they care about them, too.

Cultural change won't happen unless people at the top do it first. Until the CEO starts eating lunch in the cafeteria instead of her desk, it's a risky proposition for anyone making the leap themselves. They just have no idea whether this cultural change is actually something that's valued and will help them move up the ranks. Instead, pressure from the top has to come on people who *aren't* engaging in these activities. Not I'm-going-to-fire-you-unless-you-do-what-I-say pressure, but a steady beat of suggestions that "this is the way we do things."

Some people mingle naturally, the social butterflies that have an innate ability to chat it up with colleagues and enjoy the social side of work. These people will probably have an easier time adapting to this style of work. People who are more introverted, however, will have a tougher go.

This is where many organizations stop, worrying that they'll force people to be something they're not. My goal, however, is different. Introverts still talk to people. Companies are, after all, fundamentally about getting people to work together to accomplish something that people can't do by themselves. For anyone to do his or her job, interacting with others is necessary. It's not that people need to interact a lot more or completely change their personality, but rather that they should be interacting with the *right* people at the right time.

Maybe instead of eating lunch at our desk every day, we take one day out of the week to eat with a coworker. That's a small change, and I think we could all agree that's not much of an imposition on someone who is naturally more introverted. From a collaboration perspective, however, that one interaction can make all the difference by providing a mental model of the other person's expertise. If a problem comes up down the road, people can easily call on that expertise. They'll feel more connected to the workplace, being able to trust their coworkers just a little bit more when it comes to stressful events or work-related problems. Strengthening these relationships is essential for building the ever-more-complex workplace of the future.

In addition to doing away with this individual view of productivity, we need to get rid of the notion of the lone genius. An easy way to think of our creativity, and our impact on our colleagues as a whole, is to think about how much work we can actually get done by ourselves. Imagine you discover a way to increase your performance by 10%. Assuming you work 40 hours a week, you can end up saving 4 hours of your time every week by using this new method you've discovered. If you keep it to yourself, over one year you will end up saving about 200 hours.

But what if you shared your discovery with five of your closest coworkers? Maybe it takes you awhile to teach them this new method, say 20 hours. In that case, individually you would only save yourself 180 hours, but collectively everyone would save about 1,200 hours in that first year. On top of that, however, you've now created a community where sharing tips is expected. If everyone starts discovering different time-saving tips, suddenly each person is saving 10 or 15 hours every week. The group as a whole starts saving thousands of hours, meaning more people can help out on other projects and make more connections or come up with their own projects to work on that are radically different than anything else out there.

This is why we form organizations and why hundreds of thousands of years ago we began to develop more and more complex groups: to learn from each other, to make ourselves stronger than the sum of our parts.

Back to the Future 2

As our societies got more and more complex, our basic nature had trouble catching up. Rome arguably collapsed in large part due to its increasing reliance on a distributed mode of leadership, while in our entire ancestral history, even in early city states, we were dependent upon tightly knit relationships with our colleagues. If you wanted to be a carpenter, you had to live for 20 years with a carpenter and his family. If you wanted to be a king, you had to spend decades undergoing the same rigorous training as every other king and nobleman who came before you. You had to live in the same neighborhoods, speak the same esoteric language, and drink together.

Then suddenly this all changed. In the span of a few decades in the mid-1800s, we went from organizations built on cohesive relationships to ones where factory lines and faceless masses were the key to profit and success. More and more emphasis was placed on the importance of the factory, the importance of formal process, until only 100 years later we had completely forgotten our roots. From a biological perspective, 100 years is nothing. Biological changes take millennia to manifest themselves, and we are most certainly geared toward working in tightly knit groups.

Today, people need to be creative and able to work on complex projects, infinitely more complex than anything mankind has strived to accomplish in our entire existence. Hundreds of thousands of people must work together toward a common goal.

The factory model doesn't work in these conditions. The same factors that led to our meteoric rise now make functioning in a fast-changing world increasingly difficult.

So let's think back, only a second, really, in the grand scheme of things. Let's think back a few hundred years. Back then we mostly lived in small towns, villages where we knew the other hundred or so residents by name. We trusted each other, knew how to talk to each other, and put in the time to form a communal bond. We need many of the exact same things today.

Our minds and biology are still rooted in that time. We still have the capacity to develop deep connections with each other, to create communities within larger organizations that are seemingly too big to comprehend. It's ironic, then, that these ancient abilities are our future.

This future consists of connection, collaboration, and data, a future where we're judged not solely by our own deeds, but by that of our entire community. It's a future where age-old practices of relationship building and trust are married with the new age of data gathering that the world of sensors and digital data streams has brought forth.

This future is an exciting one, where fundamentally new measurements can enable a radically new view of management. And yet, 200 years ago this new organization wouldn't be radical. In a great paradox, the company of the future will look more and more like the company of the past.

These changes will start slowly, but the walls put up around us in recent years will soon tumble down. At first this new world of work will look old, almost ancient: bustling activity as people roam around the office, small groups stopping to chat while others continue on their way, reminiscent of town squares from long ago. In fact, they look nearly identical. There's only one thing, really, that distinguishes this workplace of the future from that of the past: a small, white badge.

Endnotes

Chapter 1

1. Bartlett, Randy. *A Practioner's Guide to Business Analytics: Using Data Analysis Tools to Improve Your Organization's Decision Making and Strategy*. New York: McGraw-Hill, 2013.

2. Duhigg, Charles. "How Companies Learn Your Secrets," *New York Times Magazine*, 2/16/2012. http://www.nytimes.com/2012/02/19/magazine/shopping-habits.html?pagewanted=1&_r=2&hp&.

Chapter 2

1. Watts, D.P. (1996). "Comparative socio-ecology of gorillas." In W.C. McGrew, L.F. Marchant, & T. Nishida, *Great Ape Societies* (pp. 16–28). New York, USA: Cambridge University Press.

2. White, F.J. (1996). "Comparative socio-ecology of Pan paniscus." In W.C. McGrew, L.F. Marchant, & T. Nishida, *Great Ape Societies* (pp. 29–41). New York, USA: Cambridge University Press.

3. Heather, Peter. *The Fall of the Roman Empire: A New History of Rome and the Barbarians.* Oxford University Press, 2007.

4. *Email.* n.d. http://en.wikipedia.org/wiki/Email (accessed February 19, 2013).

5. United States Census Bureau. *Geographic Mobility/Migration.* n.d. http://www.census.gov/hhes/migration/ (accessed December 10, 2012).

6. U.S. Department of Labor, Bureau of Labor Statistics, "Employment and Earnings," January, 2010 Annual Averages. http://www.bls.gov/opub/ee/empearn201101.pdf

7. Read more in Coontz, Stephanie. *Marriage, A History: How Love Conquered Marriage.* New York: Penguin Books, 2006.

Chapter 3

1. Zillgitt, Jeff. "Analysis: Is there a remedy for what's ailing the Miami Heat?" *USA Today*. November 24, 2010. http://www.usatoday.com/sports/basketball/nba/heat/2010-11-23-miami-heat-early-troubles_N.htm (accessed October 8, 2012).

2. Hinkin, Timothy R., and J. Bruce Tracey. "The cost of turnover." *Cornell Hotel and Restaurant Administration Quarterly* 41, no. 3 (2000): 14–21.

3. Dababneh, Awwad J, Naomi Swanson, and Richard L Shell. "Impact of added rest breaks on the productivity and well being of workers." *Ergonomics* 44, no. 2 (2001): 164–174.).

4. Roy, Donald F. "'Banana Time': Job Satisfaction and Informal Interaction." *Human Organization* 18.4 (1959): 158–168.

5. Wallace, Catriona M., Geoff Eagleson, and Robert Waldersee. "The sacrificial HR strategy in call centers." *International Journal of Service Industry Management* 11, no. 2 (2000): 174–184.

6. French, John R.P., "Field Experiments: Changing Group Productivity," in James G. Miller (Ed.), *Experiments in Social Process: A Symposium on Social Psychology,* New York: McGraw-Hill, 1950, p. 82

Chapter 4

1. Rocco, Elena. "Trust breaks down in electronic contexts but can be repaired by some initial face-to-face contact." In Proceedings of the SIGCHI conference on Human factors in computing systems, pp. 496–502. ACM Press/Addison-Wesley Publishing Co., 1998.

2. O'Leary, Michael Boyer, and Mark Mortensen. "Go (con) figure: Subgroups, imbalance, and isolates in geographically dispersed teams." *Organization Science* 21, no. 1 (2010): 115–131.

Chapter 5

1. Classified Ad 5—No Title, *New York Times*; Dec 1, 1958; ProQuest Historical Newspapers: *New York Times* (1851–2008) p. 54.

2. Jones, Del. "Some firms' fertile soil grows crop of future CEOs." *USA Today.* January 9, 2008. http://usatoday30.usatoday.com/money/companies/management/2008-01-08-ceo-companies_N.htm (accessed November 15, 2012).

3. Linebaugh, Kate. "The New GE Way: Go Deep, Not Wide." *Wall Street Journal.* March 7, 2012. http://online.wsj.com/article/SB1000142405297 0204571404577257533620536076.html (accessed August 23, 2012).

Chapter 6

1. Rhodes, Joe. "The Making of 'The Simpsons'." *Entertainment Weekly*, May 18, 1990.

2. *List of The Simpsons Episodes.* n.d. http://en.wikipedia.org/wiki/List_of_The_Simpsons_episodes#Ratings (accessed February 19, 2013).

   List of South Park Episodes. n.d. http://en.wikipedia.org/wiki/List_of_South_Park_episodes (accessed March 6, 2012).

3. Priyamvada Tripathi and Winslow Burleson. "Predicting Creativity in the Wild: Experience Sample and Sociometric Modeling of Teams." In *Proceedings of the ACM conference on Computer Supported Cooperative Work.* Seattle, WA. February 11–15, 2012.

Chapter 7

1. Gupta, Jitendra K., Chao-Hsin Lin, and Qingyan Chen. "Characterizing exhaled airflow from breathing and talking." *Indoor Air* 20, no. 1 (2010): 31–39.

Chapter 8

1. Holliday, Katie. "The 10 largest M&A deals of all time." *Investment Week.* February 8, 2012. http://www.investmentweek.co.uk/investment-week/news/2144492/the10-largest-deals.

2. Abramson, Larry. "eBay Buys Net Phone Provider Skype." *NPR.* September 13, 2005. http://www.npr.org/templates/story/story.php?storyId=4844220.

3. "Communicating the Skype way." *The Economist.* August 17, 2006.

4. "Craigslist Founder Newmark Blasts eBay Culture." *InternetNews.com*. December 11, 2009. http://www.internetnews.com/breakingnews/article. php/3852711/Craigslist+Founder+Newmark+Blasts+eBay+Culture. htm.

5. Aral, S. & Van Alstyne, M. 2007. "Network Structure & Information Advantage" Sunbelt XXVII Social Networks Conference, May 1–6, Corfu, Greece.

6. Ludwig, Sean. "Google VP: Two-thirds of our acquisitions have been successful." *VentureBeat*. May 23, 2012. http://venturebeat. com/2012/05/23/google-acquisitions-successful/.

7. "100 Best Companies to Work For." http://money.cnn.com/magazines/ fortune/best-companies/2013/snapshots/1.html?iid=bc_fl_list

Chapter 9

1. "747 Fun Facts." *Boeing*. n.d. http://www.boeing.com/commercial/ 747family/pf/pf_facts.html (accessed October 12, 2012).

2. Sosa, Manuel E., Steven D. Eppinger, and Craig M. Rowles. "Are Your Engineers Talking to Each Other When They Should." *Harvard Business Review*, 2007. http://hbr.org/web/special-collections/insight/ communication/are-your-engineers-talking-to-one-another-when-they-should

3. Daniel, Mac. "Blacksmiths keep commuters on the move." *Boston Globe*, January 24, 2007.

4. James D. Herbsleb, Kathleen M. Carley. "Socio-technical congruence: a framework for assessing the impact of technical and work dependencies on software development productivity," ESEM '08 Proceedings of the Second ACM-IEEE international symposium on Empirical software engineering and measurement, pp 2–11.

5. Benjamin N. Waber, Kate Ehrlich, and Mary Helander. "Communication Patterns in Distributed and Collocated Software Teams." 29th International Sunbelt Social Network Conference, San Diego, USA, March 2009.

Chapter 10

1. World Economic Forum. *Personal Data: The Emergence of a New Asset Class*. World Economic Forum, 2011.

Index

A

accelerometers, 9-11

acquisitions. *See* M&A (mergers and acquisitions)

aggregating data, privacy and, 19-20

airplanes

    Boeing 787 Dreamliner, 124-125, 162-163, 175

    jet engine project, complexity of, 164-165

ALS (Lou Gehrig's disease), accelerometers and, 9

Amazon.com, Kindle and disruptive innovation, 124

AOL/Time Warner merger, 151

Apple Inc, iPhones, 9-10, 124

Aral, Sinan (MIT), merger integration, 155-156

Aristotle, telescope development, 5

Arizona State University, R&D (research and development) labs study, 131-135

Asimov, Isaac, three laws of robotics, 21

assumptions

    cohesive networks, 68

    complex projects, 168

augmented cubicle project, 185-186

Augmented Social Reality, 188-189

B

badges

    batteries, 179

    evolution of, 179

    People Analytics system, moving to, 181-184

    privacy and data gathering, 179-181

    Sociometric Badges, 15-20

    UberBadges, 15

Banana Time principle, 74

Barkley, Charles, cohesive networks, 63

baseball, moneyball method, 1

basketball teams as cohesive networks, 60-63

batteries, ID cards, 179

behaviors, influencing (Target Corporation), 2-4

benchmarks (organizational), democratization of, 189-192

betweeness centrality (social networks), 54-55

bias, gathering unbiased data, 6-7

Bidi Screen, 194-195

birth predictions as analytics, Target Corporation and, 2-4

Blackberry (RIM), assumptions in cohesive networks, 68

P

R

S

W–X–Y–Z

FT Press

FINANCIAL TIMES

In an increasingly competitive world, it is quality
of thinking that gives an edge—an idea that opens new
doors, a technique that solves a problem, or an insight
that simply helps make sense of it all.

We work with leading authors in the various arenas
of business and finance to bring cutting-edge thinking
and best-learning practices to a global market.

It is our goal to create world-class print publications
and electronic products that give readers
knowledge and understanding that can then be
applied, whether studying or at work.

To find out more about our business
products, you can visit us at www.ftpress.com.